Curriculum Design in Geography

Geography Discipline Network (GDN)

Higher Education Funding Council for England
Fund for the Development of Teaching and Learning

Dissemination of Good Teaching, Learning and Assessment Practices in Geography

Aims and Outputs

The project's aim has been to identify and disseminate good practice in the teaching, learning and assessment of geography at undergraduate and taught postgraduate levels in higher education institutions.

Ten guides have been produced covering a range of methods of delivering and assessing teaching and learning:

- Teaching and Learning Issues and Managing Educational Change in Geography
- Lecturing in Geography
- Small-group Teaching in Geography
- Practicals and Laboratory Work in Geography
- Fieldwork and Dissertations in Geography
- Resource-based Learning in Geography
- Teaching and Learning Geography with Information & Communication Technologies
- Transferable Skills and Work-based Learning in Geography
- Assessment in Geography
- Curriculum Design in Geography

A resource database of effective teaching, learning and assessment practice is available on the World Wide Web, http://www.chelt.ac.uk/gdn, which contains national and international contributions. Further examples of effective practice are invited; details regarding the format of contributions are available on the Web pages. Examples should be sent to the Project Director.

Project Team

Lead site: **_Cheltenham & Gloucester College of Higher Education_**
Professor Mick Healey; Dr Phil Gravestock; Dr Jacky Birnie; Dr Kris Mason O'Connor

Consortium: **_Lancaster University_**
Dr Gordon Clark; Terry Wareham
Middlesex University
Ifan Shepherd; Professor Peter Newby
Nene — University College Northampton
Dr Ian Livingstone; Professor Hugh Matthews; Andrew Castley
Oxford Brookes University
Dr Judy Chance; Professor Alan Jenkins
Roehampton Institute London
Professor Vince Gardiner; Vaneeta D'Andrea; Shân Wareing
University College London
Dr Clive Agnew; Professor Lewis Elton
University of Manchester
Professor Michael Bradford; Catherine O'Connell
University of Plymouth
Dr Brian Chalkley; June Harwood

Advisors: Professor Graham Gibbs (_Open University, Milton Keynes_)
Professor Susan Hanson (_Clark University, USA_)
Dr Iain Hay (_Flinders University, Australia_)
Geoff Robinson (_CTI Centre for Geography, Geology and Meteorology, Leicester_)
Professor David Unwin (_Birkbeck College, London_)
Dr John Wakeford (_Lancaster University_)

Further Information

Professor Mick Healey, Project Director   Tel: +44 (0)1242 543364   Email: mhealey@chelt.ac.uk
Dr Phil Gravestock, Project Officer   Tel: +44 (0)1242 543368   Email: pgstock@chelt.ac.uk
Cheltenham & Gloucester College of Higher Education
Francis Close Hall, Swindon Road, Cheltenham, GL50 4AZ, UK   [Fax: +44 (0)1242 532997]

http://www.chelt.ac.uk/gdn

Curriculum Design in Geography

Alan Jenkins

Oxford Brookes University

Series edited by Phil Gravestock and Mick Healey
Cheltenham & Gloucester College of Higher Education

Published by:

Geography Discipline Network (GDN)
Cheltenham & Gloucester College of Higher Education
Francis Close Hall
Swindon Road
Cheltenham
Gloucestershire, UK
GL50 4AZ

Curriculum Design in Geography

ISBN: 1 86174 033 6
ISSN: 1 86174 023 9

Typeset by Phil Gravestock

Cover design by Kathryn Sharp

Printed by:

Frontier Print and Design Ltd.
Pickwick House
Chosen View Road
Cheltenham
Gloucestershire, UK

Contents

Editors' preface

This Guide is one of a series of ten produced by the Geography Discipline Network (GDN) as part of a Higher Education Funding Council for England (HEFCE) and Department of Education for Northern Ireland (DENI) Fund for the Development of Teaching and Learning (FDTL) project. The aim of the project is to disseminate good teaching, learning and assessment practices in geography at undergraduate and taught postgraduate levels in higher education institutions.

The Guides have been written primarily for lecturers and instructors of geography and related disciplines in higher education and for educational developers who work with staff and faculty in these disciplines. For a list of the other titles in this series see the information at the beginning of this Guide. Most of the issues discussed are also relevant for teachers in further education and sixth-form colleges in the UK and upper level high school teachers in other countries. A workshop has been designed to go with each of the Guides, except for the first one which provides an overview of the main teaching and learning issues facing geographers and ways of managing educational change. For details of the workshops please contact one of us. The Guides have been designed to be used independently of the workshops.

The GDN Team for this project consists of a group of geography specialists and educational developers from nine old and new universities and colleges (see list at the front of this Guide). Each Guide has been written by one of the institutional teams, usually consisting of a geographer and an educational developer. The teams planned the outline content of the Guides and these were discussed in two workshops. It was agreed that each Guide would contain an overview of good practice for the particular application, case studies including contact names and addresses, and a guide to references and resources. Moreover it was agreed that they would be written in a user-friendly style and structured so that busy lecturers could dip into them to find information and examples relevant to their needs. Within these guidelines the authors were deliberately given the freedom to develop their Guides in their own way. Each of the Guides was refereed by at least four people, including members of the Advisory Panel.

The enthusiasm of some of the authors meant that some Guides developed a life of their own and the final versions were longer than was first planned. Our view is that the material is of a high quality and that the Guides are improved by the additional content. So we saw no point in asking the authors to make major cuts for the sake of uniformity. Equally it is important that the authors of the other Guides are not criticised for keeping within the original recommended length!

Although the project's focus is primarily about disseminating good practice within the UK a deliberate attempt has been made to include examples from other countries, particularly North America and Australasia, and to write the Guides in a way which is relevant to geography staff and faculty in other countries. Some terms in common use in the UK may not be immediately apparent in other countries. For example, in North America for 'lecturer' read 'instructor' or 'professor'; for 'staff' or 'tutor' read 'faculty'; for 'postgraduate' read 'graduate'; and for 'Head of Department' read 'Department Chair'. A 'dissertation' in the

UK refers to a final year undergraduate piece of independent research work, often thought of as the most significant piece of work the students undertake; we use 'thesis' for the Masters/PhD level piece of work rather than 'dissertation' which is used in North America.

In addition to the Guides and workshops a database of good practice has been established on the World Wide Web (http://www.chelt.ac.uk/gdn). This is a developing international resource to which you are invited to contribute your own examples of interesting teaching, learning and assessment practices which are potentially transferable to other institutions. The resource database has been selected for *The Scout Report for Social Sciences*, which is funded by the National Science Foundation in the United States, and aims to identify only the best Internet resources in the world. The project's Web pages also provide an index and abstracts for the *Journal of Geography in Higher Education*. The full text of several geography educational papers and books are also included.

Running a consortium project involves a large number of people. We would particularly like to thank our many colleagues who provided details of their teaching, learning and assessment practices, many of which appear in the Guides or on the GDN database. We would also like to thank, the Project Advisers, the FDTL Co-ordinators and HEFCE FDTL staff, the leaders of the other FDTL projects, and the staff at Cheltenham and Gloucester College of Higher Education for all their help and advice. We gratefully acknowledge the support of the Conference of Heads of Geography Departments in Higher Education Institutions, the Royal Geographical Society (with the Institute of British Geographers), the Higher Education Study Group and the *Journal of Geography in Higher Education*. Finally we would like to thank the other members of the Project Team, without them this project would not have been possible. Working with them on this project has been one of the highlights of our professional careers.

Phil Gravestock and Mick Healey

Cheltenham

July 1998

All World Wide Web links quoted in this Guide were checked in July 1998. An up-to-date set of hyperlinks is available on the Geography Discipline Network Web pages at:

http://www.chelt.ac.uk/gdn

About the author

Alan Jenkins

I graduated from the geography department at UCL in 1962 and then taught in high schools in Canada and the UK. Graduate study at University of Wisconsin, Madison, in the late 1960s gave me an interest in mass higher educational systems and a training in political geography and Chinese politics. From 1975 to 1990 I taught in the geography department at Oxford Brookes University (then Oxford Polytechnic). With colleagues there we created a curriculum that focused around environmental issues, drawing on and attempting to integrate physical and human geography. We also developed teaching and assessment methods that focused on developing students as learners and by the early 1980s had created a curriculum where skills such as working in groups were central to how students learned geography. Although some of my research was on aspects of geography per se my main scholarly/ research interests was on teaching geography in higher education. With David Pepper I was co-founder and editor of the *Journal of Geography in Higher Education*, I helped set up the specialist study group in the Institute of British Geographers (IBG), and was one of the authors of *Teaching Geography in Higher Education*.

Over time my interests moved to more generic issues of teaching and learning and in 1990 I changed roles at Brookes to work in what is now the Oxford Centre for Staff and Learning Development, which is concerned with developing policies and courses for improving teaching across all disciplines at Brookes. This change of role has required and enabled me to learn much more about the literature and teaching practices in higher education. Hopefully this Guide demonstrates that there is a specialist literature and expertise regarding higher education that relates to all disciplines including geography.

However, as I have taken on this new role I have come to see that these generic issues need to be grounded in the specialist literature and concerns of the disciplines. Friendships and my own interests have also kept me in contact with geographers such as through this project and my current involvement with the Virtual Reality Field course with colleagues in the geography departments at Leicester and Birkbeck.

What I have tried to do in this Guide is to ensure that the issues and examples are firmly grounded in geography but these are set in a more generic context and draw on the expertise and scholarship in all disciplines including that on higher education. You will decide whether this is useful to you or whether I have lost contact with the worlds of geography and geographers.

1 Introduction

"I want you to imagine that you have been asked to form a new department of geography. Given the rare opportunity to write without constraint, would your curricula bear much resemblance to most of the formal courses of study to be found today? With any luck your answer will be something like, good grief no! If your answer is something else…there is not much hope for the future!

(Gould, 1973, p.253)

Great gobbets of facts are purveyed in traditional courses, and it is hardly surprising that they stick in the throats of students, particularly the intelligent ones. Learning large quantities of facts and being required to regurgitate them by multiple choice examinations (USA) or by waffle ignorance-cloaking essays (Europe) is not going to help students tomorrow."

(Gould, 1973, p.260)

"The most effective (geography) curricula are those with a definite progressive development through each stage of the course. There is appropriate progression in the level of demands placed on students between years one and two and in core areas between years two and three."

(Geography Departments) "recognise the frequent tensions between the conflicting aims of breadth and coverage. For example, a few aim to integrate human and physical geography and, hence, sacrifice some depth of study to achieve the required breadth; on the other hand, those that provide research-based courses, offer depth at the expense of breadth."

"Most institutions provide some opportunities to study elements of human and physical geography, but programmes that claim to integrate them are rare and even fewer actually match that claim."

(HEFCE, 1995a, pp.3-7).

1.1 Outline of this Guide

As the Contents page indicates I start with an overview of the curriculum, setting out its meaning and importance and the political context in which we design geography curricula.

Section 2 sets out a model of curriculum design through the analogy of an ouija board, where the curriculum is seen as shaped by a range of forces which we seek to control. Section 3 analyses these factors in more detail, with brief descriptions of geography and related curricula that embody these principles. Section 4 considers the curricula of four departments in some detail, in each case focusing on a key principle that has shaped that curriculum, for example, staff research interests; integrating physical and human geography. The focus is on the undergraduate curriculum as that is the 'core activity' of most departments, though the basic principles can be applied to the growing number of taught postgraduate courses.

This Guide is mainly addressed to a course team. For as a department we can achieve so much more by collectively ensuring that the courses designed by individuals add up to a coherent whole. While the main focus is at the level of a course team or geography department, many of the ideas and suggestions can be adopted by individuals. In a brief conclusion I offer suggestions on how to take forward the ideas that you find appropriate. At the end of this Guide there is a list of further sources, including the Geography Discipline Network (GDN) World Wide Web (WWW) pages, which contain further examples of innovative and effective ways to design geography curricula. I hope that prompted by this Guide you will add accounts to the WWW pages that both illustrate the principles I identified and add others that you think appropriate.

Like all writers I have had to struggle to find a style appropriate to the subject matter and those who will read it. The GDN project seeks to shape practice by spreading ideas which will assist other geographers to reflect upon and improve their teaching. This Guide contains a range of practical ideas and short descriptions of innovative curricula from which you can select and adapt to your context. However, at times this Guide is written in what is intended as a scholarly and somewhat discursive style. I think this appropriate because the 'sub-text' of my argument is that designing a curriculum is a piece of scholarship. Just as when we are teaching the discipline we need to be fully aware of the scholarship and current debates in the discipline, so when we help students to know and do geography, we should do so in a way that demonstrates that we are scholars in the current literature and conversations on teaching. Well that is the curriculum presented to you here - what you make of it, well perhaps that's another curriculum!

1.2 What do we mean by curriculum?

> *"The curriculum on paper is only a script: the real curriculum is acted out and lived through. Thus, in a sense, we can say that the lecturer is also a kind of content, and so are the methods he or she uses, the department he or she works in and, last but not least, the assessment that is made."*

> *(Squires, 1987, p.170)*

The dictionary definition of curriculum as "a course of study" (Concise Oxford Dictionary) is a good starting point. However, while revealing, this definition fails to identify key aspects. Another way to grasp the meaning of curriculum is to contrast it with the more limited term syllabus: "The syllabus specifies the course title and sketches the content areas to be covered, with perhaps the amount of time to be allotted to the different elements, and the main books to be used." (Gold *et al.*, 1991, p.195).

By contrast, the term 'curriculum' clearly recognises the importance of the disciplinary content and methodology, the geography that is to be learned, but goes much beyond that content to recognise that what the student learns is shaped by many factors, including: the resources available; the people teaching; the teaching and assessment methods. Indeed, many would argue that the key to understanding the curriculum that the students learn is in how they interpret the way they are assessed.

There are other wider contextual factors shaping the curriculum that students experience. Trow (1976) and Parlett (1977) identify the department, its 'learning milieu', its atmosphere, and its values, as profoundly shaping both what students immediately learn and what is remembered years later. For example, some years back a review of the geography curriculum at University College London (UCL) picked up "a departmental tradition of individualism in research as well as in teaching, only partly related to the diverse nature of the subject matter" (Wood, 1980, p.1). First year students had picked up from staff comments "the latent hostility between physical and human geographers which they detected beneath the surface bonhomie". Thus the curriculum is not just what would appear in official documents, as it was probably intended by the staff. It is also (in part) the curriculum the students are learning and experiencing. In a memorable phrase Snyder (1971) has referred to this as the 'hidden curriculum', in that it is a curriculum of which staff are often unaware. Further examples include the feminist critiques of geography curricula that fail to adequately include women's experience, or where certain GIS/quantitative or physical geography courses are experienced as masculine, technocentric territories (McDowell, 1992).

Thus when considering the curriculum we need to identify:

- the curriculum which is intended by staff and designed before the student enters the course;

- the curriculum that is delivered by the staff/learning materials (including books and software);

- the curriculum that the student learns and experiences;

- the curriculum that the student makes part of herself/himself and remembers and uses some years later.

Also, more prosaically, we need to consider the level of analysis at which we define the curriculum. Is it an individual module or course, a programme of study that is part of the degree or the whole degree itself? In this Guide I move back and forth between the level of the individual module or course and a geography degree programme, for in many cases the issues to be considered in designing a degree also need to be considered in constructing an individual module.

Furthermore, some American writers emphasize the importance of what they term the 'co-curriculum' (Graff, 1991) — the wider student life outside the formal curriculum, whether it be participating in student societies or working to pay the way through college. What is learned is profoundly shaped by these wider factors.

It is this complexity and the intellectual challenges it poses, that makes curriculum design so exciting and so important, and the challenge varies according to whether our focus is at the level of the individual teacher constructing a specialist module or on the whole geography department designing a new geography degree or revising a current one.

1.3 Why curriculum design matters

Curriculum design matters because it enables us to:

- put to the centre of our teaching our fascination with geography and the particular view of geography we possess;

- build into our teaching — should we choose — our research interests;

- design the curriculum in a way that recognises the resource constraints we face; in a context where there are so many demands on our time, we can design the curriculum to ensure we can also do the other things we want and/or are required to do;

- help students develop their knowledge and abilities as geographers and develop the skills and dispositions that will make them lifelong learners and/or develop the skills that will enable them to succeed in employment;

- design the curriculum in a way that is attractive to students and gets them to choose to join the geography programme and to stay in it; for many of us our jobs now depend upon such decisions;

- meet the increased and specific demands for internal and external quality assurance through the way we design and present the curriculum;

The above issues are later considered in detail, but first I consider these requirements for accountability.

1.4 The political context of curriculum design

> *"There is no consensus that UK degrees are broadly comparable with one another. What is needed are means by which the level, purposes and standards of programmes and qualifications they lead to can be plotted in relation to each other and to agreed benchmarks."*
>
> *(HEQC, 1997c, p.1)*

'Accountability', 'assessment', 'outcomes measurement', 'performance funding': these are some of the key words that Sydney Jumper (1992, p.94) of the Geography Department, University of Tennessee, associated with the "then recent (sometimes politically motivated) efforts to encourage colleges and universities to evaluate their performance" in the USA. In 1997, French government proposals for the reform of higher education included: moves to core courses, particularly in the first year; the establishment of a national committee for the evaluation of research; moves to more clearly link the university curriculum to industry and commerce; the rights of students to assess teacher performance (HEQC, 1997a).

While the first draft of this Guide was written just as the Dearing proposals for the review of UK higher education was published (National Committee of Inquiry into Higher Education, 1997), I purposefully do not look at the details of these recommendations, for it was known that they would be replaced by a Government White Paper which, in turn, will be followed by some other measure. Rather, I stand back from the Dearing recommendations and set out what are seen as the more deep-seated aspects of the political context of curriculum design, in the European Union (including the UK!), North America and Australasia. The central argument is that in designing a geography curriculum these political forces have to be recognised: they don't have to be valued. We may wish to join with Joe Powell (1990) in resisting what he sees as the 'corporate management paradigm' and its impact on (Australian) geography. However, it is in a department's interest to ensure that certain (senior) staff have the responsibility to make themselves aware of likely government initiatives in higher education and to suggest ways the curriculum can be designed or presented to recognise these pressures or to be 'protected' from them.

The key political trends that define the context in which geography curricula are designed include governments, and organisations close to government, which have intervened and will continue to intervene, to determine funding, direction and purpose of higher education. There are a variety of reasons for this, including the (perceived) importance of higher education to wealth creation and the cost to the tax-payer of providing that education. This, in turn, results in the 'massification' of higher education, with attendant calls for efficiency gains and attempts to introduce performance indicators and performance funding, including, in the UK, the Research Assessment Exercise (RAE) and Teaching Quality Assessment (TQA). It has also resulted in increased class sizes and 'deteriorating' student:staff ratios in UK geography departments (Jenkins & Smith, 1993) with attendant pressures for the curriculum to be designed to cope with these factors (Sections 3.3 and 3.4). Similar trends are noted in a recent analysis of Australian geography (Rich *et al.*, 1997).

As more of the costs of this expansion shift to students, including the increasing number of mature students, so there are pressures to ensure that the curriculum meets their (perceived) needs (Section 3.8).

Governments, funding bodies, corporate organisations and students themselves, pressure higher education to better ensure that the curriculum produces a skilled work force. There are then attendant requirements/encouragements to ensure that geography curricula include transferable skills and links with industry (Chalkley & Harwood, 1998), and also to prioritize those areas of the discipline, for example, GIS, that are clearly relevant to employment.

As higher education moves from being a positional good of a restricted elite to becoming a 'mass' commodity, funded from public and private funds, so there are increased concerns for the quality of the 'product'. Recently, in the UK, this has taken the cultural form of an emphasis on the 'gold standard' of the quality of the honours degree and concerns about the variability of standards of degree classification by disciplines and institutions. Research by Keith Chapman (1994) of the Department of Geography, University of Aberdeen, on degree results in British geography has played a key role in this debate. In the USA, where there are no such cultural assumptions about common standards across varied institutions or departments, there are related requirements for institutions and departments to be able to verify their own standards, and for the assessment at both institutional and departmental levels be designed to deliver those standards. In the UK there has been much debate (HEQC, 1997b) about whether there should/can be national, discipline-based and/or institutional and departmental standards for degree 'standards'. This was also a theme of the Dearing Report which called for a new external review process based around a strengthened external examiner system to be in place by 2000. In March 1998 this hardened into a consultation paper from the new Quality Assurance Agency "An Agenda for Quality" (QAA, 1998). In brief the key features of the proposed quality assurance methodology are:

- A move away from the TQA model of an investigation of the teaching and learning process, which included observing teaching.

- A requirement for all programmes (for example, the geography curriculum in your department) to set out their course to a common framework (see Figure 1 — note that this is a draft framework[1]). This information will be publicly available on the WWW and it is assumed that students will use this to help decide the institution/ course they apply for.

- A focus on outcomes, for example a specification of the knowledge and skills that students will be able to know/do as a result of studying geography in your department.

- A national qualifications framework, with level descriptors, for example a specification of what can be expected/required of geography graduates.

- This qualifications framework will be linked to subject benchmark information in order to provide a broad statement of what is expected at the threshold level in an academic discipline. Geography is one of the 41 subject areas in the draft framework.

- Verification of these levels and standards through registered external examiners (perhaps in part trained through discipline-based organisations such as the Royal Geographical Society with the Institute of British Geographers (RGS-IBG).

Clearly this tells us in the UK the political context in which we will have to state (if not necessarily design) our curricula. Designing our curriculum in part around this framework might include: defining the core outcomes that we would expect graduating students to achieve (see Section 3.6) and then to rigorously determine the assessment methods used across a degree programme to ensure that students could achieve those outcomes (Section 3.7). Reference here should be made to the Guide on '*Assessment in Geography*' in this series (Bradford & O'Connell, 1998). We might also ensure that we follow Chapman (1994; 1996) in researching our assessment practices and degree results to better ensure we had documented evidence of our degree standards and perhaps student perceptions of the assessment methods used on their course (see Section 3.10).

---

[1] *UK readers should ensure that they have the 'current' methodology. This can be obtained from the Quality Assurance Agency for Higher Education (QAA), Southgate House, Southgate Street, Gloucester, GL1 1UB. Tel: 01452 557000. http:// www.qaa.ac.uk.*

Figure 1: *Illustrative example of a completed programme specification template, for Applied Geology at Oxford Brookes University (from Jackson, 1997)*

1. Award BSc (hons)	*2. Programme Title* Applied Geology	*3. UCAS Code* F610	*4. Programme Type* Single subject - modular

5. Main Purposes
To develop the intellectual and practical skills of the learner in the acquisition and understanding of geoscience data in preparation for: i)   a career in geoscience-based industries or education ii)   non-specific employment iii)   life-long learning and an appreciation of the value of education to society

6. What a graduate should know and be able to do on completion of the programme

To successfully gain the award the student will have demonstrated: i) subject knowledge and understanding; ii) cognitive skills; iii) subject-related practical or professional skills and iv) key skills and other transferable skills as specified in the learning outcomes for approved modules in the programme. Further details are available at http://www.brookes.ac.uk/schools/sces/courses/appgeo.html

1. subject knowledge and understanding, e.g.
- geological principles, terms, definitions & classifications
- the structure, composition and history of the earth & timescales
- geological processes and their role in shaping the Earth
- the structure and properties of Earth materials
- the fossil record and the evolution of life
- Earth's natural resources and the techniques used to locate and exploit them
- the role of the geologist in society with regard to economic development and environmental sustainability

2. cognitive skills, e.g.
- demonstrate the skills necessary to plan, conduct and report a programme of original research
- synthesize information/data from a variety of sources
- analyze, evaluate/interpret geological data
- apply geological principles and methodologies to the solution of problems
- extrapolate information from two- to three-dimensions
- formulate and test concepts and hypotheses

3. subject specific skills, e.g.
- observe, record accurately & account for geological features in the laboratory and the field
- demonstrate the skills involved in the preparation and interpretation of geological maps and cross sections from field observations and other sources of information
- prepare descriptive and interpretive technical reports
- use field and laboratory equipment competently and safely to acquire geological data

4. key (transferable) skills, e.g.
- capacity to learn (in familiar/unfamiliar situations)
- communicate effectively (written, verbal, graphical...)
- numerical skills appropriate to the geoscientist
- competent use of Information Technology (e.g. WP, WWW, databases, spreadsheets, specialist packages)
- able to work as part of a team

7. General Attributes Profile

The twenty most important skills and capabilities developed and assessed through the programme are indicated on the profile. The programme may also support the development of other personal qualities, skills and attributes through its educational goals.

A Intellectual	B Practical	C Personal	D Social/interpersonal
critical reasoning	research skills & methods	independence/self-reliance	cooperatively
understand and apply concepts	laboratory practical skills	self-motivation	teamwork
problem solving	field craft skills	planning and organisational skills	communication
analysis & interpretation	information processing skills	enterprise and resourcefulness	environmental awareness safety conscious
integration of knowledge strands	observation and recording skills	able to learn independently and	
data synthesis			

---

8. Main Subjects, Levels, Credits & Qualifications

All modules have a credit rating of 15 except for the two double modules which are worth 30 credits.
1 credit is equivalent to 10 notional hours learning (class contact + independent study)

BSc hons degree
360 credits

HE level 4

compulsory module
- applied geology fieldwork
- applied geology project (30)

option modules
- environmental geochemistry
- major earth structures & tectonics
- basin analysis

- energy resource geology
- mineral resource geology
- exploration & evaluation of geological resources
- applied hydrogeology
- geophysics
- advanced studies

option modules taught at either level 2 or 4
- **micropalaeontology and palynology**
- **oceanography**
- **hydrology**
- **water resources**
- **Quaternary geomorphology**
- **remote sensing**
- **principles of geotechnics**
- **soil mechanics**
- **rock mechanics**

HE Diploma
240 credits

HE level 2

compulsory module
- geological fieldwork

option modules
- the fossil record
- igneous petrology
- structural geology

- metamorphic petrology
- geochemistry
- geophysics

HE Certificate
120 credits

HE level 1

compulsory modules
- introduction to geology
- fundamentals of mineralogy and petrology (30)
- ancient environments
- environmental geology
- introductory geological fieldwork

recommended modules
- introductory chemistry
- microcomputer applications
- introduction to statistics
- environmental sustainability
- introduction to topographic mapping
- basic mathematical methods

This element of the specification shows the levels at which subjects are taught and assessed (the level structure is that given in the NCIHE Report). It also provides information on the credits that can be gained for learning that has been assessed and the intermediate qualifications that can be gained if a learner choses to interrupt their studies.

---

9. Assessment Process

- assessment criteria linked to learning outcomes for each module
- overall ratio of coursework : unseen examination 50:50
- assessment points at the end of each term
- minimum pass mark 40%
- assessment methods (number of modules using each method)
  - unseen written examinations (25)
  - laboratory practical tests, reports and workshops (16)
  - field exercises and reports (6)
  - essays and technical reports (9)
  - poster displays and illustrated charts (5)
  - teamwork simulations of exploration programmes (4)
  - independent project and dissertations (2)
  - oral presentations by individuals and project teams (6)
  - simulated research applications and consultancy reports (3)
  - assembly of resource bases using Web (3)
  - Web page presentations (1)
  - open book exams (2)

This element of the specification shows how the outcomes described in box 6 and 7 are assessed. The numbers in brackets indicate the number of times that a particular method is used in a typical programme.

10. Standard Referents

- entry standards are comparable to those for similar programmes in other post-1992 universities
  - typical entry requirements is 2 C grades at A level in appropriate subjects or advanced GNVQ/BTEC equivalent
  - mature students can enter via APL/APEL or foundation science year
- programme has been established for x years; last revalidation by university in 1996-validation panel included an applied geologist from a post-1992 university and a geologist from industry
- the programme will be submitted for accreditation by the Professional Body (the Geological Society)
- recent external examiners have been from the University of Wales and Leeds, and from the British Geological Survey
- the current external examiner is from the University of Oxford

This element of the specification provides information on the entry standards and the external reference points that are used by the department to position the standards in the award.

However, just as governments are intervening to shape teaching and learning, so there are similar, and sometimes perhaps contradictory, pressures for research performance and accountability. In the UK and Australasia there are pressures for departments to gain external research and consultancy income on the US pattern. This, in turn, asks hard questions about how the undergraduate curriculum can be managed to ensure that staff have time to do research. Responses to this might include carefully costing the curriculum (Section 3.3) and, more explicitly, linking the curriculum to staff research (see Section 3.2 and the case study of the geography department at UCL in Section 4.2).

In addition, there are wider political and economic changes: in particular, the impact of globalisation and the role of information technology. Some UK geographers (for example, Bradford, 1996; Unwin, 1997) fear that the Government may intervene as they have done at school level to legislate for core curricula to ensure 'standards'. I consider that a far more fundamental attraction to governments, institutions, departments and commercial bodies will be the national and world-wide provision of core materials. These could result in a *de facto* national or international curriculum. One possible response to that is for geographers at a national and even international level to co-operate to produce and disseminate materials that reflect their agenda (see the case study of the Virtual Geography Department in Section 4.4, and also the geography curriculum projects in the list of WWW sites).

Clearly, readers may see different political forces, or interpret them differently than I have here. While starting from this political context it is not the intention to prioritize it; I certainly hope that readers will wish to design their curricula with a focus on the values of geography as a discipline (Section 3.1), the specifically educational concerns and theories of student learning (Section 3.5) and the research evidence of the impact of the curriculum on student learning (Section 3.10). To anticipate Section 2, I argue that effective curriculum design involves recognising and giving priority to the factors we 'choose'. However, that choice needs to be informed by our knowledge of the discipline, of the literature on curriculum design and on the political context in which we work. For those of us in the UK these factors are, in part, brought together in the judgements of the TQA assessors of geography curricula, considered in the next section.

1.5 Teaching quality assessment (TQA) assessors and geography curricula

UK geographers will be well aware of the TQA methodology for the assessment in 1994-95 of the quality of higher education provided by geography departments in England and Northern Ireland, and the similar methodologies used in Scotland and Wales. In brief, departments were required to assess themselves as excellent, satisfactory or unsatisfactory and to write a statement justifying that claim. Subject assessors (largely geographers) then studied those documents, selectively visited institutions to talk to staff and students, to see students' work and visit classrooms and followed this up with a written public assessment of the quality of teaching in that department (for further details and discussions of this exercise see HEFCE, 1995a; HEFCE 1995b; Chalkley, 1996; Johnston, 1996; Healey, 1997). The overall report and all the assessments of the individual geography departments are on the funding council's WWW site http://back.niss.ac.uk/education/hefce/qar/geography.html.

Clearly, this is a very particular example of the political context of curriculum design discussed in the previous section. It is also — at least in the UK — an external-defined methodology that is now being replaced by a new methodology with a focus on degree standards (Section 1.4).

The approach here, while recognising the limitations of the methodology — it's a series of snapshots by subject experts with limited training in assessing teaching quality — is to see it as a valuable source on the perceived quality of geography curricula. It provides a unique, large scale source on geography curricula and an informed view by discipline specialists of the strengths and weaknesses of geography curricula at that time. In particular, it provides a lens through which we can view the curriculum in our department (and that department could be in North America or Australasia) to see if it directs us to particular ways to redesign it. This account draws heavily upon the subject overview report for geography (HEFCE, 1995a), the individual department reports (see WWW site above) and an analysis by de Vries (1996) of some of those assessments for geography (and other disciplines). In reading this analysis we suggest that, as a department or as an individual, we consider how we should judge the 'effectiveness' of our own curriculum against these (explicit) views of 'quality'.

The perceived strengths of geography curricula

The subject overview saw the then strengths of these geography curricula as:

- "Clearly articulated aims and objectives, which are carried through into curricula and syllabuses."

- "Students have a wide choice (between departments) ranging from highly specialised courses offering a relatively narrow cover in great depth to those offering considerable breadth of study."

- "Syllabuses are generally up to date and include recent developments in the subject, including those in GIS and remote sensing."

- "The link between teaching, scholarship and research is highly valued in geography and staff research interests frequently enrich the curriculum."

- "The most effective curricula are those with a definite progressive development through each stage of the course. There is appropriate progression in the level of demands placed on students between years one and two and in core areas between years two and three."

- "In addition, there has been a growing commitment to providing students with transferable skills related to subsequent employment."

(HEFCE, 1995a, pp.3-6)

The perceived weaknesses of geography curricula

The subject overview saw the then weaknesses of these geography curricula as:

- (Departments) "recognise the frequent tensions between the conflicting aims of breadth and coverage. For example, a few aim to integrate human and physical geography and, hence, sacrifice some depth of study to achieve the required breadth; on the other hand, those that provide research-based courses, offer depth at the expense of breadth."

- "Most institutions provide some opportunities to study elements of human and physical geography, but programmes that claim to integrate them are rare and even fewer actually match that claim."

- "Where modularization has been introduced, there have been some problems in addressing all of the stated objectives within such a framework."

- "In geography the evidence of (curricula) development from year one to year two is generally clear but is less convincing thereafter."

- "Although compulsory elements and the final year dissertation present additional challenges, option subjects in year two and three are not substantially different in their level or the demands they impose on students."

- "In some of the more flexible modular programmes, students can avoid advancing their technical skills (e.g. GIS) beyond the introductory level."

- "In some 30 percent of departments visited, a coherent (transferable) skills programme has yet to be established. In these cases, skills are more likely to be acquired incidentally rather than through a carefully designed strategy. Furthermore, there were examples of employers being consulted on the appropriateness of the curriculum. Most students learning experiences are not strongly permeated by direct contact with, or experience of, the world of work."

- "Where students take geography as part of a joint or combined studies, they sometimes do not enjoy parity of opportunity with the generally much larger group of honours students. Examples include lack of access to fieldwork, pastoral support, project work and the acquisition of transferable skills. There is also a lack of integration between the subject areas in many joint degree schemes."

(HEFCE, 1995a, pp.6-7)

1.5.1   What about the sub-text?

These then are the overall public judgments. Clearly these were shaped by the external political requirements on the assessors to use a particular methodology, that is to have no external view of quality but to judge a department's curriculum against its particular stated aims and objectives — see Section 3.6. De Vries (1996) doubted that such staff would be so neutral in their assessments, noting that the assessors "were mainly academics themselves — subject specialists…people likely to be steeped in academic culture, and bearing with them their own ideological baggage, norms, criteria and the like of what constituted quality in HE." His hypothesis was that these norms would clearly come into their judgements. His way of uncovering these values was a careful analysis of the detailed departmental reports for a range of disciplines, including geography. He argues that in effect assessors, whatever the stated methodology, were judging these departments against deep-seated academic views of quality, including: the currency of the disciplinary knowledge presented to students; whether there was clear evidence of academic progression and whether the various elements of the curriculum clearly cohered together.

We need not stay any longer with this interpretation of the TQA, for even in the UK it is to be replaced by another methodology. What is significant and of international relevance about de Vries' analysis is that in developing our own curricula we are expressing our values and that when we are to be assessed by others, from within our own institution or outside, we need to decode the values by which we will be judged.

2 Overview

2.1 The ouija model of curriculum design

Ouija board *"Board lettered with alphabet and other signs, used with movable pointer to obtain messages in spiritualistic seances."*

(Concise Oxford Dictionary)

Some educational theorists and some university managers and quality bodies consider there is one best or required way to design a curriculum. While recognising the value of some of these methodologies, for of course there is not just one such algorithm, that is not the approach adopted here. Instead I suggest that either as an individual, or as a geography department, it is helpful to conceive curriculum design through the metaphor of an ouija board, for at times the curriculum is going to be shaped by forces over which we have little control and often little warning; that is the political context in which many of us work — see Section 1.4. Starting from the metaphor of an ouija board as something moved by mysterious forces, I see the curriculum as being moved by a set of forces which we both recognise and shape. These forces become strategies for designing the curriculum. Naturally, different departments and individuals in different institutions will give greater value to certain forces, and at particular times certain forces may become more prominent. Thus the curriculum is never fixed but is continually being reshaped.

The particular forces identified are shown in Figure 2 (overleaf) and briefly introduced in the next section. Many of them are explored in Section 3 with respect to brief descriptions of particular geography curricula. Section 4 examines, in detail, the curriculum of four Geography Departments.

Figure 2 identifies the range of forces or strategies that geographers need to both recognise and shape when designing a curriculum. Certain forces, for example, the potential of distance-based learning technologies, both paper- and courseware-based, are considered in other Guides in this series.

Before reading this overview you may want to complete the questionnaire in Figure 3 at the end of this section. Alternatively, read the overview and then do the questionnaire before considering particular strategies or forces in detail.

2.2 An overview of curriculum design

External quality requirements

The importance of this issue and the likely factors that need to be considered was discussed in Sections 1.4 and 1.5. Here I simply state that it is politically important to recognise what is required and what is seen as good practice by external and internal quality organisations.

At their best these requirements can identify educational issues that should be addressed. More strategically one can adjust the curriculum, including its presentation, to achieve what is required and/or what will give us advantages, such as resources. For example, in some universities different allocations of resources go to those courses that are defined as science- or laboratory-based. Thus, the Department of Geography at the University of Alabama was faced by university committees threatening the laboratory status of its introductory physical geography courses. However, by adjusting those courses to ensure they included 'hands on experimentation', which was the key determinant of how the university defined a laboratory course, the department managed to meet the requirements of these key committees and hold on to the resources it wanted (Lineback & Harlin, 1987).

In adopting this strategy it is necessary to begin by identifying who are the key actors inside and outside the university with (political) power over the curriculum: their relative influence; what credence we wish to give to their values; identify how they expect or require the curriculum to be described; what issues have to be addressed; and then construct the curriculum to recognise, if not necessarily value, these realities.

The discipline (see Section 3.1)

What are the central features of the discipline that we want to present to students? What do we consider is so important about geography, that students should be unable to graduate without having studied it, or had the opportunity to do so? We also have to decide whether to present a single integrated view of the discipline or a curriculum where many methodologies and viewpoints collide and compete. We have to decide how to conceive and present the relationship between physical and human geography and incorporate research methods and specialist techniques into the curriculum.

Figure 2: *The ouija model of course design*

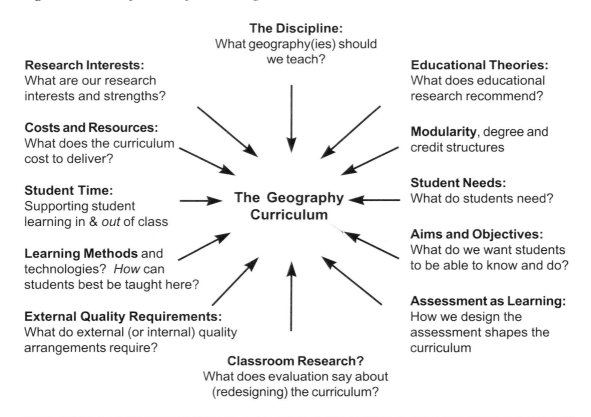

Research interests (see Section 3.2)

Many of us individually want to make an explicit link between our teaching and research interests. In many departments the view of quality teaching is one which is explicitly research-based, both in terms of content and in developing a department with a clear research culture. Recognising the force of this push, this strategy identifies how staff research interests can feed into the curriculum. It also identifies ways in which a research-oriented culture and practice can be developed amongst students. This issue is also considered in the case study of UCL (Section 4.2).

Costs and resources (see Section 3.3)

Recognising and working from our research interests and disciplinary concerns determines what we want to do. By focusing on costs and resources we emphasise the importance of what we can afford to do, and accordingly shift the curriculum in that direction.

We start by identifying the resources we have, in particular the critical variable of staff time. We also identify what the current or intended curriculum costs to run, and work through alternative possible curricula to identify the curriculum we choose to afford. In adopting this approach we are careful to identify the full range of resources available to us, including support staff and the skills of our students.

Student time (see Section 3.4)

Traditionally curriculum design has focused on what staff and students do inside class. Perhaps a better approach is to focus on the time we can require and expect students to learn, both outside and inside class. Having identified that time we focus on designing learning and assessment activities to use that time productively. Time in class is then seen as one means, albeit limited, to direct and support learning outside class.

Learning methods and technologies

In supporting student learning inside and outside class, we need to identify what teaching methods are most appropriate (for example, lectures, seminars, fieldwork) and what is their most effective balance and inter-relation. We also need to give increasing attention to those learning methods, whether they be paper or courseware, that support student learning outside class and perhaps at a distance. This issue is not discussed in detail here as other Guides in this series, in particular those on '*Resource-based Learning in Geography*' (Healey, 1998) and '*Teaching and Learning Geography with Information and Communication Technologies*' (Shepherd, 1998) cover this territory. Here, I discuss particular aspects in further detail in the Sections 3.4 and 3.6 and in the detailed case study of the Virtual Geography Department (Section 4.4).

Educational theories (see Section 3.5)

It is important to consider key educational theories which illuminate how students learn most effectively and which as geographers we can use to develop curricula which can produce high level learning. In particular I look at four key theories or models. In 'deep and surface learning' a basic difference is recognised in how students approach their studies, between a 'deep approach' when students focus on meaning and understanding, and 'surface learning' where their approach is to focus on low level replication. In 'experiential learning'

I see individuals as having certain preferred learning styles and in designing the curriculum we shape it to systematically develop all these styles. I then consider 'mastery-based learning' or Keller-plan style courses where the curriculum is divided into small units, which the students have to pass or master, before moving on to the next element of the curriculum. Finally, I see students as constructing meaning, at times 'incorrectly' and analyse how the curriculum can be designed so they develop understanding that is an accurate representation of the world.

Aims and objectives (see Section 3.6)

One powerful approach to curriculum design is for staff to identify the aims and objectives of the curriculum, for example, what do they want students to be able to know and do as a result of studying geography in a department. This outcome-based approach can then lead to carefully defining the assessment that will both support students and ascertain whether and to what level they have achieved these outcomes. It can also lead to identifying the teaching and learning methods that support the objectives we have decided upon (or, of course, those that have been externally determined for us). This objective-based approach is, in part, based on theories of student learning and has significantly shaped what external quality organisations require in how we present the curriculum.

A department assessment strategy (see Section 3.7)

It is not unusual for assessment to be considered as a final bolt-on element to the curriculum. The content is decided, the books specified, and then finally and often much later, the assessment tasks are specified. A radical approach to curriculum design is to start by asking what evidence (assessment tasks) could students present to demonstrate that they had reached the levels of knowledge and abilities that we consider appropriate? Having agreed on, for example, the assessment criteria for a first class degree and the assessment tasks that would determine whether these levels have been achieved, one moves to determine the teaching methods to be used and the content to be covered. This approach to curriculum design is most clearly demonstrated at Alverno College, Milwaukee, with its philosophy of "assessment as learning" (Alverno College Faculty, 1994) (http://www.alverno.edu/). The detailed case study of Liverpool Hope University College (Section 4.1) reveals how its curriculum is shaped by Alverno. How a department might approach curriculum design through assessment strategy is discussed in Section 3.7. A separate Guide in this series (Bradford & O'Connell, 1998) provides a range of suggestions on particular methods of assessment (for example, assessing groups).

Student needs (see Section 3.8)

What do students need from the geography curricula that we design? Clearly this is an increasingly important force to be recognised, as students now pay an increasing percentage of the costs of their education and have more choice of where and how to study. It is also an area where governments are intervening to shape the curricula in ways they consider meet student needs; or perhaps more what governments need graduating students to be able to do! In this section I focus on defining those needs, in particular considering issues of life-long learning and employability, and indicate how geography curricula have been and can be designed to meet student needs.

Modular and credit structures (see Section 3.9)

One force that most of us now clearly recognise is the impact of the modular or credit structure within which most UK geography curricula are now designed. In this section I consider how we can use that structure to meet what we consider to be the needs of our students, to give time for us to do such things as research. In short, while recognising that the (modular) degree structure does in part direct the curriculum, we can recognise and use it to direct the curriculum in ways we consider appropriate.

'Classroom' research (see Section 3.10)

But perhaps the ultimate force we have to consider is what is the end result of all this effort? What impact does the curricula we have devised have upon our students? What do they make of it? How can we evaluate our courses to find out? While recognising the value of end-of-module evaluations, here I recommend ways of bringing a research culture to our teaching and asking harder and more useful questions, and with this information consider how we can best redesign the curricula.

Clearly these forces are not watertight categories. For example, our sense of what is worth teaching in geography is likely to be shaped by our research interests, and the aims and objectives we set for the curriculum will no doubt reflect what we perceive as our students' needs. However, when considered separately, they each illuminate particular issues and give us strategies to design the curriculum to reflect what we see as their relative power to address our particular circumstances. Seeing the curriculum as an interplay between these forces also implies that there is no single place to start. You should read, and more importantly use, the more detailed explication which follows in the order you think appropriate. Perhaps having read this overview, now is the time to reconsider or complete the questionnaire in Figure 3 (overleaf).

Figure 3:   *Curriculum questionnaire*

Please complete this questionnaire by ticking the box which most closely accords with your views

Statement	With respect to the current geography curriculum in this department					With respect to the geography curriculum I would like to see created in this department				
	Strongly disagree	Disagree	Neither agree nor disagree	Agree	Strongly agree	Strongly disagree	Disagree	Neither agree nor disagree	Agree	Strongly agree
The curriculum is closely based upon staff research interests										
Students are able to specialise in the aspects of geography that interest them										
Students graduate with little or no ability to do geographic research										
Students graduate with little understanding of the inter-relation between physical and human geography										
The teaching of GIS/quantitative techniques is clearly integrated into the overall geography curriculum										
We have adequate staff resources to deliver the curriculum										
We have adequate technical/capital resources to deliver the curriculum										
The curriculum shows inadequate recognition of issues of gender or ethnicity										
The curriculum prioritises staff conceptions of what and how students should study										
There is a coherent departmental assessment strategy										

Please complete this questionnaire by ticking the box which most closely accords with your views	With respect to the current geography curriculum in this department	With respect to the geography curriculum I would like to see created in this department
	Strongly disagree / Disagree / Neither agree nor disagree / Agree / Strongly agree	Strongly disagree / Disagree / Neither agree nor disagree / Agree / Strongly agree
The curriculum focuses on supporting student learning outside class		
The curriculum fails to develop in students the skills that will make them lifelong learners		
The curriculum equips students with transferable skills that will aid their employability		
We have no clear explicit requirements for what constitutes a first, second… or fail degree in geography		
We specify, in a language that is clear to potential employers, what geography graduates know and can do		
The curriculum is unaffected or redesigned by how students experience the curriculum		
The curriculum is clearly shaped by theories of how students learn		
The curriculum fully capitalises on the institution's (modular) degree structure in which we work		
Fieldwork/field courses are clearly integrated into other areas of the curriculum		

3 Explication

3.1 Building the curriculum around our conception(s) of geography

"Every discipline includes, implicitly or explicitly, some value commitments about what is worth studying and how it should be studied."

(Dressel & Marcus, 1982, On Teaching and Learning in College, p.95)

"Today's distinctive environmental consciousness, and the requirements of the National Curriculum in geography that partly stem from it, make it more important than ever for geographers to tackle the research problems on the common ground where human and physical geography overlap."

(Cook, 1992, p.131)

"The principal training of a geographer should come, wherever possible, by doing fieldwork."

(Sauer, 1956, p.296)

In designing a curriculum, either as individuals or as a department, our initial and probably, central concern is with the content: the geography we think worth teaching. While other sections of this Guide offer a range of, hopefully, practical suggestions, that is not the main approach taken here. Most readers will be experts in the discipline and also will work in particular departments, with staff with particular specialisations and views of the discipline. Rather, the approach is to set out what are seen as the central questions individuals and, in particular, departments face in designing their geography curriculum.

> What individuals/departments can do is to consider the questions/issues set out below and use them to interrogate:
> * the curriculum that is now delivered;
> * the curriculum that we wish to see developed;
> * if relevant, what key changes to the design of the curriculum should be instituted.
>
> In considering this we should ask what we can do as individuals, or with a limited number of colleagues, and what needs to be done at the level of the whole department?

There is a growing research interest in what Becher (1989) has called 'disciplinary cultures', that is, the particular epistemologies, truth criteria and practices of the disciplinary community. Becher's original formulation considered this issue for particular disciplines, including history, physics and a brief mention of geography, solely in terms of their *research* interests. Others have taken this concept and applied it to the *teaching* of particular disciplines. For example, both Evans (1993) and Thomas (1990) have looked at the issues of teaching and learning 'English Studies' as perceived by teachers and students. Thus both show how issues of gender can shape, and are shaped by, the discipline and its pedagogy. As yet no-one has done such a research-based study for geography in higher education. However, there are many articles (often presidential addresses) written by geographers on their views of the curriculum, and it is these articles, along with our practice in designing geography curricula, that are drawn on to formulate the questions proposed above.

3.1.1   A metaphor: geography as conversation

Bob Kirk (1995, p.269), head of the Department of Geography at the University of Canterbury, New Zealand, when his department was going through a major curriculum review likened the challenge to that formulated by Blair Kinsman's (1965) study of ocean waves:

In one respect "and one that is of very practical concern to the beginner, science is a conversation. The conversation has been in progress for a long time — in the case of ocean waves, for a very long time. To make the analogy more exact, science resembles the babble at a very large reception… The participants in the conversation have sorted themselves into groups, sub groups and sub groups, each dominated by a few brilliant conversationalists who set the subject and tone. Some scientists wander from group to group, while others remain fixed. Some groups talk about similar things, and occasionally snaps of conversation pass from one group to another. **You have arrived in the middle of a party… My job is to catch you up on the conversation and show you how to find your way to the bar.**" (emphasis added).

Kirk (1995, p.270) argues that "applied to curriculum design the analogy suggests that the variety and mix of learning situations experienced should foster the transition from 'hearing' to more steadily informed 'speaking' and 'listening', and should confer progressively more greater independence of learning. A good way to begin is to expose students to as wide a range of conversations going on in groups and subgroups as possible."

3.1.2   Particular conceptions

What is the particular conception(s) of geography as a discipline held by staff in the department? Is there agreement on one overriding view of the discipline? Or, rather, do we take the philosophical position that such a single view is neither possible nor desirable, either at a research level or at the level of the undergraduate curriculum? For, clearly, it is possible to formulate a conception of the discipline at the research frontier, which may be different from our sense of what is distinctly valuable about its role in an undergraduate education.

This meta-question, in itself, poses further questions particularly concerning the relationship between physical and human geography and the value of particular methodologies of inquiry/knowing. As geography has developed as an academic discipline in the UK, the long-standing debate in both pronouncements on the curriculum and its practice is how we conceive and present to students the relationship between human and physical geography. I recall the comments of the TQA assessors (Section 1.5) that "most institutions provide some opportunities to study elements of both physical and human geography, but programmes that claim to integrate them are rare and even fewer actually match that claim" (HEFCE, 1995a, p.6). Is this because we consider this an impossible or undesirable aim or that, as yet, few departments have developed curricula structures that deliver that aim. For one such attempt see the case study of Oxford Brookes University (Section 4.3).

Perhaps as geography departments link together, or co-locate, staff with research interests related to physical sciences, humanities and social sciences, they can present a wide range of research methodologies to students. As academics we may want to celebrate this wide variety of geographical imaginations. While we may also think that this offers particular opportunities in curriculum design in presenting to students contrasting ways of knowing the world, this also opens up a major problem in curriculum design, for educational research suggests the importance of students having a clear map or knowledge base on which to build new knowledge (see Section 3.10). In designing a geography curriculum that celebrates different ways of knowing, we have the challenge of building that structure and then questioning it and helping students to make sense of, and use, these contrasting methodologies (Phillips & Healey, 1996).

What is the overall purpose of a geography education at undergraduate level? Clearly this will be shaped by both our particular conceptions of geography and our 'political' view of the purpose of education. Is its particular value seen as contributing to the broad goals of liberal education? Or do we take a socially reformist view of its value, as does McDowell (1992, p.248) and see its role as preparing students "to be active citizens, able to think critically and struggle against social injustice in various locations." Or, perhaps, do we emphasise to students the social practice and ecologically based value of the discipline and its contribution to environmental understanding and action (O'Riordan, 1996). Such questions clearly relate to our views of students' needs (see Section 3.8). In that context we may wish to prioritise those aspects of the discipline, including its use of a wide range of research methodologies and its strength in both the knowledge and application of GIS techniques, that will help students in a highly competitive job market. Or with David Smith (1995, p.282) would we see students needs as including a "systematic exposure to moral thinking."?

3.1.3   Only connect

The nature of geography as a discipline presents further opportunities and problems in curriculum design. These include:

- Geographers in their research and teaching interests have strong links with cognate disciplines. Many would agree that it is at these frontiers that the important research questions are posed and where a dynamic curriculum can be presented to students (Jackson, 1996). This creates a challenge to those of us teaching systematic options, for we have both to find ways of connecting geography students to other specialist areas (and this could be in a 9-15 teaching week modular course — See Section 3.9) while connecting these different disciplines to students' developing conception of geography.

- There is the related problem of connecting students' understanding of these systematic, and perhaps regional, options with any core, whether that core be methodological (see the case study of UCL, Section 4.2) or around an integrated physical/human core as at Oxford Brookes University (Section 4.3).

- As a discipline, geography deals with phenomena in both time and space, and at a variety of scales. Handling this complexity is its strength in what it can offer students. However, without careful curriculum design it can just open up a bewildering and poorly understood set of disconnected ideas and facts. To return to the analogy of curriculum design as conversation, all students get to hear is a babble of poorly understood discordant voices.

Suggestions for departmental action:

- Present students with a clear conception of the discipline and its methodologies. That conception may be one that presents and celebrates a diversity of potentially competing perspectives.

- Ensure that, within the constraints and opportunities of your degree structure, students are inducted into these perspectives at an early stage, and are then returned at various points in the course to develop, challenge and elaborate on the perspectives.

- Ensure that the curriculum clearly connects students' knowledge of geography with the technical and analytical tools to understand and contribute to the conversations in the discipline. For example, if with Carl Sauer (1956) you consider that "The principal training of a geographer should come, wherever possible, by doing fieldwork", then students will see that in the curriculum structure, content and methods of assessment.

- Rigorously research to see whether, at the end of the course, students have understood and appreciated these perspectives. One way to do this would be for semi-structured interviews with selected graduating students.

3.2 Research interests: linking (staff) research and the curriculum

"There was clear evidence of scholarship and research activity having a beneficial impact on teaching and learning in around half of the providers visited."

(HEFCE, 1995a, p.9)

Many individuals want to pursue and link both teaching and research. Certain departments want to develop a research-led curriculum, for that is their view of quality (see the case study of University College London, Section 4.2, and compare it with that of Liverpool Hope University College, Section 4.1, where the focus is on value added, with more of a skills- and life-transforming focus to the curriculum).

This section offers suggestions to individuals and departments who wish to develop a research focus to the curriculum, and link the undergraduate curriculum with staff research, I offer the cautionary observation that this research focus is but one way of designing the curriculum. Perhaps more fundamentally the research evidence on the linkages between research and teaching "have failed to establish the connection between the two" (Brew & Boud, 1995, p.261). My view is that the two can be connected to produce a beneficial impact on teaching and learning, but it has to be done systematically, while ensuring that the disadvantages of this approach, in particular staff not being available to meet student needs, are minimised. Although there are some things that individuals can do, it is appropriate here to concentrate at departmental level, because to minimise the disadvantages of a research-led approach does require collective staff action. Furthermore, while recognising the supreme importance to quality teaching of what Boyer (1990) and others have called the 'scholarship of teaching', or an awareness of the debates and the current literature of the discipline and on teaching methods, the focus here is on how Boyer's 'scholarship of inquiry' or original research, particularly that of staff in the department, can have positive impacts on the curriculum.

3.2.1   Developing student awareness of geographic research

Students often arrive from school or college with a view of knowledge being fixed, written and codified in textbooks. Perhaps a central goal of higher education is to make them aware that knowledge is not fixed: it is socially created. We want to design the curriculum to ensure that students appreciate the nature of scholarly enquiry and be able to understand and conduct research studies. Strategies for this include:

- Make it central to the first year curriculum: don't leave it till upper level courses. For example, Dartmouth College, New Hampshire, requires all first year students to take a 'First Year Seminar' (Barff, 1995). This is representative of programmes in many US institutions, which recognise that much of first year teaching in year one is in large classes, where much of the teaching is carried out by teaching assistants and where assessment is often by objective tests. Many US and Canadian institutions now require, or guarantee, all first year students at least one course which is taught by experienced staff, in a small discussion format, and with emphasis on library inquiry and assessed course work.

- While many such programmes focus on learning to learn skills (as does the seminar programme at Liverpool Hope University College, Section 4.1), many of these first year courses at Dartmouth are ones which are closely based on the teachers' research interests.

- John Bryson (1997) at Birmingham University developed a first year tutorial programme that centred around a critical reflection of a popular 'A-level' geography textbook. In effect such a programme is acculturating these students to the different view of knowledge that is required at undergraduate level.

- At the Department of Geography at UCL, all first year students interview individual staff about their research interests and the linkage with their teaching (see Section 4.2).

- Develop modules or courses where the focus is less on the geography *per se*, but more on an analysis of the process of enquiry.

- Develop modules or courses where the content is closely based around the research interests of staff, either as individuals or research groups (see Section 4.2).

- Develop modules or courses which acquaint students with the contract nature of much contemporary research, and that designing a research proposal involves a careful specification/awareness of the costs involved. See, for example, the assessed exercises developed by physical geographers at Oxford Brookes University which require students to design and cost a research proposal (http://www.lgu.ac.uk/deliberations/geography/trans_index.html); or consider the computer-based simulation *Soil Surveyor*, where students construct a soil map of an area, but every time they 'dig' a proportion of their finite budget is debited (Dawson *et al.*, 1995).

- Consider how the co-curriculum (the informal curriculum — see Section 1.2), develops and supports students' awareness of geographic/staff research. Ways to do this include developing a student geography society with invited speakers (we could credit student work and learning through this society, and limit our workload by crediting it — see Sections 3.3 and 3.9). Make students informally aware of the research activities in the department by poster displays on completed or current staff research projects and by bulletin boards displaying recent publications.

- Invite former students back to the department who are now employed in industry and elsewhere as researchers, to talk about their jobs and effectively to demonstrate to students that a curriculum focused on staff research can support student employability. Also develop strong department links with research-based firms and organisations. Such an approach might require a much stronger link with employers' organisations than many geography departments have yet developed (see the GDN Guide by Chalkley & Harwood, 1998). Such linkages, or the lack of them, are one part of the curriculum we design.

3.2.2   Developing students' ability to do geographic research

- Develop compulsory core modules which progressively develop students' ability to plan and carry out a geographical investigation. Both the detailed studies of UCL and Liverpool Hope University College offer examples of this approach; indeed they are a feature of many geography departments.

- Make an individually executed large scale investigation a compulsory requirement for honours graduation. Such dissertation courses are common features of many UK geography departments (see the GDN Guide by Livingstone *et al.*, 1998).

- Selectively weight the dissertation/research elements of the degree to signal its importance to students. For example, the Department of Geographical Sciences at the University of Plymouth weights the project as 6 modules out of the 36 required for graduation.

- Provide credited opportunities for students to participate in staff-led research projects.

- Provide effective formal and informal links with postgraduate students so that undergraduates are aware both of postgraduate research projects and of the nature and potential of postgraduate research.

Linking teaching and research at Southampton University
(for further details, see entry by David Martin on the GDN WWW pages,
http://www.chelt.ac.uk/gdn/abstracts/a74.htm)

The Southampton department has as one of its strategic objectives 'to maintain excellence and innovation in research-led teaching'. The department's curriculum has been designed to achieve this through the following:

- While the first year of the course necessarily provides a broad-based geographical education, opportunities are sought to bring students into contact with departmental research by drawing on current research as exemplars in basic courses. In the Wessex field course students carry out project work relating to active departmental research in the local region, such as hydrological work in the New Forest Research Catchment.

- In the second and third years there is an emphasis on option courses which are closely aligned with the department's six research themes, and which are frequently taught by small teams of staff from within each theme. Many of these courses are strongly linked to current research. For example, courses in GIS and spatial data handling in which the computer practicals are directly derived from recent staff research projects in population modelling and geostatistics.

- Postgraduate students are actively involved in fieldwork, practical and seminar classes, providing further opportunities for students to build bridges between class-based foundation teaching and current departmental research.

- The undergraduate research project is seen as a key component of the Southampton course (worth 16% of the final degree classifiable marks), with students encouraged to undertake projects aligned with the department's research themes.

- Close links with departmental research also allows students to take advantage of facilities such as the Wolfson-funded laboratories for GIS, remote sensing, quaternary and fluvial research.

3.2.3   Protecting staff time to do research

Research and teaching can be symbiotic activities, as indicated above, but they compete for that all important variable: staff time. Given that in most state systems governments are requiring 'efficiency gains' of universities, most departments face the acute dilemma of delivering more, including the undergraduate curriculum and research outputs, with less staff time. This dilemma should be recognised. One broad strategy is to deliver the curriculum in ways that protect staff time to do research. The case study of UCL (Section 4.2) in part illustrates this approach. Specific strategies that departments can develop include:

- Carefully costing the curriculum in ways that effectively use all the resources available including student time out of class (see Sections 3.3 and 3.4).

- Designing the curriculum that guarantees all staff a regular period of limited or no teaching. For example, at Oxford Brookes University (see Section 4.3) geography is taught in a three term modular course. A major review of the curriculum started from a design principle that all staff would have one term per year with no formal teaching except for personal tutoring and dissertation supervision. All an individual's teaching would be concentrated in two terms. This clearly requires a careful balancing to ensure that these 'light terms' were equally spread amongst the three terms and that all core courses could be effectively taught. It also means that staff have higher teaching loads in the other two terms; but that is considered a price worth paying to get uninterrupted time to do research.

- Using a range of resources to meet student needs but to protect academic staff from continued demands on their time, including, course booklets, a departmental Intranet, support staff and student guiders (see Section 3.3).

- Developing a departmental policy of fixed office hours, and developing a culture and policy that this is the only time that students should see staff out of class.

3.2.4   Limit the disadvantages of staff involvement in research

There are dangers and disadvantages in developing a research-led curriculum and one that is based around staff's research interests, including protecting their time to do research. This section draws on current research at Oxford Brookes University which is investigating, across a range of disciplines, student perceptions of staff research (Jenkins *et al.*, 1998). The key problems students have identified about the formal and informal curriculum, that were shaped by staff research interests, included: staff involvement in research meant that they were not available and often at key periods, for example, in the Easter vacation just as students were completing their dissertation (a key part of the curriculum); a perception that staff were not interested in students and teaching, while for these undergraduates the central function of the university was quality teaching. A research ethos was part of that conception of teaching quality, but only part. Good communication skills, approachability, an interest in students and availability outside class were the staff qualities that were more firmly stated. There is a danger in a research focused curriculum, resulting in the situation identified by the Association of American Geographers, where staff pick up the message that "earning tenure, promotion and salary increases have hinged largely on research productivity" (Abler *et al.*, 1994, p.9). These are the conditions which prompt students to pick up the 'hidden curriculum' that undergraduate teaching doesn't matter.

Strategies for limiting the disadvantages of focusing the curriculum around staff research interests include:

- Make sure that there are clear effective mechanisms for students getting advice and consulting staff outside class. The use of office hours, bulletin boards and email can all ensure that students experience support in learning outside the formal teaching periods.

- Making a periodic evaluation (Section 3.10) to check that students perceive these strategies are effective.

- Individual staff can both protect their own time and ensure that students feel supported by devoting specific time in class to identify the problems that students are having with the course, for example, 'I can only afford *x* office hours per week to deal with your queries. I realise that may not be enough to deal with all your concerns. Assume each of you had individually fifteen minutes with me. What 3 key problems or issues would you want explained or advice upon. You have the next 5 minutes to write them down and hand them in anonymously. At the beginning of the next session I will deal with the main issues you identified.'. This strategy will pick out major recurrent problems and ensure they are dealt with effectively and efficiently.

Some of the main findings of the current research at Oxford Brookes University include the fact that many students are totally unaware of what research staff are doing, are not informed of why staff are away, or what research they are doing. Many are unaware of the contractual and financial reasons why research is carried on at the university. Strategies for dealing with these aspects of the 'hidden curriculum' include:

- Providing information in the university prospectus, department guides for students, and through staff-student consultative committees to make students aware of why certain staff are heavily involved in research, and the perceived benefits to students of this involvement.

- Make sure that students are fully aware, well in advance, of when staff are to be away doing research and describe what research they will be doing. On return let students know the results of that research, for example, through poster displays.

There is a danger that curriculum around specific staff research interests will devalue, in both staff and student eyes, those courses that are more integrative in nature; these may be compulsory core courses. There is a danger that the main experience of students, particularly in the vital first year with evident danger of heavy drop out rates, will be courses over which staff have little concern or involvement. One might counter that through:

- targeting more resources to those courses, including administrative support, laboratory time and so on;

- making explicit deals in a department where the teaching of research-led modules, sabbaticals, and so on, is conditional upon specified effective involvement in core courses;

- making these core courses the responsibility of specific staff, who see their careers and interests in such courses, but then ensuring that the rewards of sabbaticals and promotions support these staff.

In short, developing a research-led focus to the curriculum is partly about the construction of specific modules, course structures and department practices. It is also very much about creating a departmental culture and hidden curriculum that ensures that this is to the students' benefit.

3.3 Costs and resources

"Few institutions collect data on fieldwork costs in a systematic and rigorous way, or are able to monitor and compare financial and other inputs to fieldwork in a constant way."

(DES, 1992, p.4)

'It's daft not to use the main resource we have, the skills and knowledge of our students.'

Sections 3.1 and 3.2 have emphasised what we want to do in building a curriculum, including a view of what geography has to offer students and our particular research interests. Here the focus is different: we concentrate on what we can afford to do, carefully identifying the costs of alternative curriculum designs, and also identifying the full range of resources, particularly student time, and the skills of support staff, we potentially have to resource the curriculum.

3.3.1 Costing the curriculum

This issue has to be analysed at three different levels: the institution (which is beyond our control); the geography department and the individual. I can indicate only the issues and possible methodologies, for different institutions have different ways of identifying and costing departments for particular services, for example, only a few explicitly charge to departments the costs of rooms, heating and media services. As many institutions move to devolved budgeting the particular institutional budget arrangements will shape what aspects of the curriculum individual departments have to consider costing. Given those costing arrangements departments should map out alternative curriculum designs and decide what they can afford.

Because staff costs represent the largest component of most departmental budgets, and because our time as individual lecturers is the most scarce resource we have, academic staff time needs to be central to curriculum design. Most of these issues have to be resolved at the level of the whole department, and clearly department heads have a major role here. However, there are things that individual lecturers can do.

3.3.2   Cost your module

As an individual, consider a particular module or course you teach and calculate the time it took you to teach the module last year. Factor into that cost the time taken to design that module when you first taught it. Now think about alternative course designs for the module. What would they cost you in time? Table 1 below may prove useful, or you may think it misses out key costs and issues. If so redesign it and then cost your module. Gibbs (1992c) provides a range of hypothetical costs for a range of courses in a variety of disciplines. The particular issues of costing fieldwork and laboratory teaching are considered in Jenkins (1997) and Gibbs *et al.* (1997).

Table 1:   *Costing a module*

Current Design	No. of hours	Alternative Design	No. of hours
Estimated cost of original design		Estimated cost of course redesign	
Estimated preparation time		Estimated preparation time	
Hours in classroom teaching:		Hours in classroom teaching:	
Lecturing		Lecturing	
Seminars/ laboratories		Seminars/ laboratories	
Fieldwork (include travel time)		Fieldwork (include travel time)	
Hours marking:		Hours marking:	
course work		course work	
exams		exams	
Office Hours		Office Hours	
Cost of teaching module		Cost of teaching module	
Cost of teaching module (divided by 5? to indicate likely 'life span' of module).		Cost of teaching module (divided by 5? to indicate likely 'life span' of module).	

It might be prudent to consider the cost of teaching your present module assuming a 20% increase in student numbers, with no increase in the time you can allocate to the module; that may be the realistic scenario you are faced with. It is likely that the key change in such a costing will be the time taken to assess the module. In that respect the key change you can make to your curriculum is to radically reconsider the way the course is assessed (see the GDN Guide by Bradford & O'Connell, 1998). Remember that the way students are assessed is probably the key determinant in what they learn. Another option you can consider is radically shifting the balance of the curriculum and your time to supporting student learning out of class (see Section 3.4), then cost the time required to redesign that module and ensure that time is used to support student learning.

3.3.3 Costing a departmental curriculum

Our focus, as at the level of the individual module, is largely on the staff hours necessary to teach the curriculum; this is a factor which all staff will recognise, while department managers know the staff budget is a central concern. However, at the level of the department we also concentrate on the number of students taught on particular modules, the number of learning hours and the Credit Accumulation Transfer System (CATS) credits they generate (somewhat equivalent to Carnegie units in the USA).

In the UK a student studying a course full-time is expected to spent 1200 hours studying — the equivalent of studying 40 hours a week for 30 weeks. This is a national 'standard' and is the basis for CATS units. These provide a somewhat crude but powerful way for a department to cost its current curriculum, the workload of individuals and to consider alternative models of course redesign.

An example of a module costed this way (after Gibbs, unpublished paper) is:

- a 15-week long module, taught by two lectures and a seminar each week for twelve weeks;
- assessment is by two essays and an unseen examination;
- it enrols 80 students;
- it costs 235 hours to teach and assess;
- at this institution full-time students are required to do eight modules.

A full year of study is equal to 120 CATS units so this module is weighted at $120 \div 8 = 15$ CATS units (or 120 learning hours). So the cost of this module is therefore $235 \div 80 \div 15 = 0.2$ lecturer hours per student per CATS unit. While by comparison the figures for the other 17 modules offered by the department are…

Clearly these are hypothetical figures and as a department you might want to change the weighting depending on module size and other factors, but it provides a consistent clear methodology for a department to cost the curriculum.

Using this methodology does not assume or require that all modules should produce the same CATS credits or student learning hours. There are good reasons why certain modules or areas of the curriculum should get increased resources. Departments may well choose to target scarce resources to particular areas, for example, fieldwork modules, honours dissertations, core compulsory modules or, as in the case study of Liverpool Hope University College (Section 4.1), the first year. What is proposed here is that these should be considered choices, made with full awareness of the real costs involved, and that to target such resources is a statement of what is valued and what has to be supported by cheaper modules elsewhere. Finally, when a department redesigns its curriculum it is helpful at an early stage to cost alternative speculative redesigns.

It is useful not only to identify the full costs of teaching the curriculum, but also to identify the full resources available to deliver that curriculum; clearly in large measure that is the time and knowledge of academics (Sections 3.1 and 3.2). However, it is also possible to consider the role of support staff and student time more systematically.

3.3.4   Valuing support staff

Those of us who are regular readers of *The Times Higher Education Supplement* know how the mythical media studies department of the University of Poppelton is effectively managed, and where students are largely supported and taught by the secretary Maureen, while Professor Lapping and Dr Piercemuller are elsewhere. Some of us may identify these fictional scenarios with geography departments we know.

Building a curriculum that is shaped by effective valuing of all staff, underpinned by an equal opportunities commitment, might mean recognising and valuing the contributions of support staff, possibly by changes in job titles and payment. Furthermore, it is likely that shifts to increased use of resource-based learning and information technology will, as with other industries (for example, banking), threaten the clear job demarcations and salary structures that exist in most universities. Clearly there are trade union considerations here, but in redesigning your curriculum you can choose to explicitly consider how your entire staff might be used in a more effective way to support the curriculum. As an indication of what can be done, here are 'anonymous' sketches, based on real geography departments world-wide, to indicate directions you might take. Many of them were probably introduced for managerial reasons to reduce costs, however, they promise an increase in the quality of delivery to students. Furthermore, they create increased job opportunities and pay for support staff:

- As one lecturer took early retirement, s/he was replaced by a desk-top publisher (at a lower salary) and the difference in salary was used each year to redesign a compulsory module to make more use of learning packages.

- Teaching-only staff, with no requirement or support to do research, were hired to teach the first year programme. This represented a 30 per cent reduction in the salary costs of teaching the first year programme. As those hired were mainly former school teachers this represented increased pay and job satisfaction for them.

- As secretaries were replaced, academic staff were required to do their own typing. Over five years the 6 department secretaries were replaced by 3 course administrators. They took over much of the management of courses, including student induction and student advising. The overall budget costs remained constant.

- In a large department with a strong commitment to laboratory-based teaching, 3 of the 7 technicians were enrolled in the university-wide course for postgraduate teaching assistants and on a Masters programme in geography. Their job title and pay was changed as they were given increased responsibility for teaching on first year laboratory courses. If this proves successful it is hoped to extend the scheme to upper level courses.

- A department appointed a student links co-ordinator who was a recent graduate from the department. S/he was responsible for, and had a budget for, developing a scheme where selected third year students were paid to run an induction programme for first year students. Academic staff thus had only limited specified responsibilities for academic advising in the first year.

- A department decreed that the staff development budget, including sabbaticals, should be 'annually reviewed to ensure that there was equitable, but not necessarily equal, consideration of the role of support staff'. An annual target of 30% of the total staff budget was an indicative figure of the allocation to support staff.

3.3.5 Using and recognising students skills and knowledge

Much of the 'hidden curriculum' consists of the informal support and teaching that students offer each other. Here I consider how this can be made explicit. I am not considering the role of postgraduate students taking on aspects of teaching; here I consider how undergraduate students can be used to support each other.

- The Department of Geography at the University of Liverpool set up a resource centre with key articles and materials for students to study outside 'class'. It is run by a small group of second and third year geography students who are paid for their work. They are chosen by student groups, making a competitive presentation as to why they should be selected.

- Paul Browning of the Department of Geology at the University of Bristol has experimented with using students to convert lecture notes and slides into WWW pages. This enables students to study when they wished and for him to teach a course that made limited use of formal lectures.

  Having secured funds for vacation salaries from a University Teaching & Learning: Excellence & Innovation Fund, he emailed all second and third year students listing a series of Uniform Resource Locators (URLs) where they would learn to put material on the WWW using HyperText Markup Language (HTML). This skill was not part of the formal curriculum. By way of an application for the job students were invited to submit their CVs (consisting of text and an image of themselves) via the WWW.

  The students were self-selecting; those that were able to teach themselves HTML and learn how to publish their CV on the Web had mastered the skills to do the task required and were given a summer job! Most of the material the students produced hides behind an Intranet; however, one example is "Minerals and the Microscope" which can be found at http://www.bris.ac.uk/Depts/Geol/opmin/mins.html.

These are but two examples of a general approach to formally use and pay for the knowledge and skills of undergraduate students, to support the learning of other students. I deliberately started this section by illustrating the principle with examples of students being paid for the activity. Though some of us may reject this 'commercial' approach it does both dramatise the issue and offer an approach to curriculum design that we can choose from. There is US research which indicates that where students also work for money, their grades are less threatened and even improved when they work on campus. Certainly the two examples above are things a student is both likely to learn from and gain something for their CV.

An alternative way of paying students for supporting the learning of others is to credit it. The boxed snapshots below include examples of this approach. In some institutions students who act as course representatives can gather portfolio evidence of their learning to get academic credit.

Snapshots of supplemental instruction in geography

Supplemental instruction (SI) was developed at the University of Missouri, Kansas. It has been adopted in many disciplines world-wide. SI uses students, and pays them by money or credit, to support the learning of other students. Originally developed for high-risk courses, for example, large first year courses with high drop out rates, the original approach has been adapted to other contexts. Usually there is an academic staff co-ordinator and students are not responsible for formally instructing other students, rather they are trained to support informal classroom sessions with other students by asking questions and getting students to work with others. Typically the student guiders are upper-level students who have taken that module in a previous year. Generally, students who attend their sessions do so on an optional basis, and sessions typically start by then defining the difficulties they are facing. Research indicates positive impacts on grades both for those attending and the student helpers. Examples of UK geography departments that have used this approach are:

- University of Central Lancashire — David Longworth (1994) credited upper-level geography students for assisting on a course on IT for first year geography undergraduates.

- St Mary's University College Stuart Oliver (1995) trained and paid students to assist a minority of students having difficulties with IT (see also http://www.chelt.ac.uk/gdn/abstracts/a22.htm).

- University College London — second year students were trained to support first year students in statistics practicals.

Note that the projects at St Mary's University College and UCL have been discontinued, partly because the central university Enterprise programme that paid for it has ended.

Paying and/or crediting the work and learning students do to support the curriculum are perhaps beyond what many of us consider feasible or appropriate. 'Softer' ways of formally using the skills and knowledge of students to support the learning of others, and themselves, include:

- front loading the curriculum in stage one to give students the skills and knowledge to work with limited staff support in upper-level courses (see Sections 3.4 and 4.2);

- developing, through explicit teaching, students' ability to assess their work and/or that of their peers (see the GDN Guide by Bradford & O'Connell, 1998);

- developing students' ability to work in learning teams or groups, to support learning in and out of class (see the GDN Guide by Chalkley & Harwood, 1998);

- encouraging the development of unpaid 'buddy-systems' in which second year students are paired with first year students (and third year student with second year students) to induct them into core elements of the curriculum, to help them in designing their programme, and to help them with aspects such as computing. While such 'mentoring' can last the year it may be more effective when targeted at key times of the year, or at specific activities;

- developing mechanisms and curricula where students build on the learning of others. That is what we do as researchers; our students seldom have that opportunity explicitly built into the curriculum. One such example is Edinburgh 2003, where second year students are building upon the fieldwork research of student fieldwork in previous years to build up a picture of longitudinal change (Smith, 1995).

Not only do these approaches of using students save staff time and can cut departmental costs, if well managed they can also further develop students' knowledge and skills and give them achievements they can put on their CVs. After all we are better geographers, and are paid to become so, through the experience of teaching others!

3.4 Student time: time in class and time out of class

'Lectures are like sermons, it is what people do between them that matters.'

Curriculum design has often focused on what happens in class, with an implicit focus on what lecturers do. By contrast, an approach that focuses on total study time shifts the design process to supporting student learning outside class, with the classroom sessions seen as one important way of supporting that learning.

3.4.1   Student learning hours

How many hours a week does your department or institution expect a full-time student to work both in and out of class? Is that agreed amongst staff, and is the curriculum designed on that basis? Is that made clear to students? Such factors are often left implicit. In this approach these issues are explicitly addressed and made central to the design process.

In the UK the CATS is based around students studying 1200 hours, or 40 hours per week, for 30 weeks. Research in the UK and elsewhere has indicated that full-time students can productively spend 40-45 hours per week studying and that there are important differences between disciplines in the amount of that time that is spent in class. Thus, humanities classes tend to have limited classroom contact whereas engineering classes have high contact hours. More recent research has indicated that in some first year courses which emphasise mass lectures and end-of-course unseen examinations, students can spend as little as 20 hours studying per week. They and many upper-level students are now spending an increasing proportion of the week in paid employment, with negative consequences for their grades and their learning. The above is a crude summary of research on a complex area, but hopefully demonstrates the importance of focusing the design process on time in class and out of class.

To indicate how this can be done, look at the description of the course below, from the Geography Unit at Oxford Brookes University where all single modules are designed around 150 hours of student learning.

Geography and the Contemporary World

Teaching and learning methods:

This module (a second year compulsory module) is designed on the assumption that students will spend their 150 hours in the following ways:

Term 1

In class:	15 hours of introduction to fieldwork area and project options
In class:	4 hours of consultation in a project group with staff project supervisor
Out of class:	20 hours planning, reading and preparation (including two draft and assessed fieldwork proposals)
'Vacation':	56 hours of fieldwork

Term 2

Out of class:	40 hours of background reading, group discussion and writing final report
Out of class:	10 hours preparing group presentation
In class:	5 hours giving a presentation and attending and contributing to the assessment of other project groups

Assessment

This module is 100% course work, of which 80% is where students are assessed as a group and 20% is on an individual exercise.

Term 1

10% for project plan 1
10% for revised project plan
Fieldwork/vacation: 20% for individual field journal

Term 2

10% oral presentation
50% for final report

3.4.2   A health warning

In some institutions and departments, using phrases such as 'student-centred learning', elements of this approach have been adopted to try to cope with budget cuts. Librarians faced with 200 first year geography students, divided by their tutors into teams of 6 and all 'researching' a topic for which the library does not have adequate resources, know this strategy as BOFO (bugger off and find out...). The critical point to emphasise is that this strategy emphasises the importance of *supporting* student learning outside class.

3.4.3   A departmental strategy

Ways in which a department can develop this strategy:

- Require all modules/courses to have a common number of student learning hours, and specify how those hours are to be divided between in and out of class activities.

- Develop an explicit strategy for students who can work independently or in teams (Gibbs, 1992b; Gibbs, 1994b). This should not be left till the third year dissertation or project courses, but should be progressively developed through the degree. What happens in the first year is particularly important in developing a student culture of supported independent learning.

- Ensure that student learning out of class is resourced, for example, through the way that the department's space is laid out to enable independent and group learning, by a policy of required and monitored office hours, through targeting x% of the departmental budget to support paper and IT resource-based learning (see the GDN Guide by Healey, 1998).

- Make this strategy explicit to students; this probably needs to be central to stage one of the course, but will need to be repeated and developed.

- Research how students spend their time, and act upon that research (see Section 3.10).

3.4.4   Individual lecturers

Individual lecturers can develop this approach by thinking of an individual module as an iceberg: what's beneath the surface (for example, out of class learning) is most important. Practically, you can:

- even if the department will not require all courses to be specified in learning hours and time in and out of class, individual staff can do that, make it explicit to students and research how students spend their time on their module;

- construct a course as a time line (and make this explicit to students) where classroom sessions punctuate and support learning outside class;

- (radically) rethink the role of lectures (Jenkins, 1992) and seminars, so that their focus is on supporting what students do after the session and may well require students to prepare for classroom sessions;

- ensure that the assessment system supports this design; this may involve some assessed course work which require students to prepare for classroom sessions.

Overleaf are brief descriptions of this approach, which we may want to adapt.

Using assessment to support learning before a class session

See these examples as indicative of an approach: for example, you may not want to use the same precise methods. However, you may want to adopt the principle and develop methods you think appropriate.

Require pre-class work, e.g. reading or problems to be solved, and then open the session with a five minute test on that work. The teacher can mark it or students could be trained to quickly mark their peer's work. If appropriate by using (computer-marked) objective tests the work can be quickly marked by teacher or students. For an excellent example of an engineering problem-solving class taught using this broad strategy see Forbes & Spence (1991). Here, in a problem solving class with 170 students taught largely by lectures, exam results were poor and students did not complete the recommended, but not required, out of class problem-solving exercises. Staff did not have time to mark the out of class exercises out of class! One key change was made to the course: students had to complete 50 problem-solving exercises out of class and these were peer-assessed in six staff-supervised peer marking sessions which were part of the normal lecture slot. Student's out of class work significantly increased, staff workload remained constant and assessment results, including the unseen examination, significantly improved.

- As a variation on this approach, David Pepper of the Geography Unit at Oxford Brookes University requires students to summarise their notes on assigned pre-seminar reading. At the end of the seminar he marks their notes on a 1-5 scale, according to whether they have met five stated criteria.

- Recommend students to individually summarise pre-reading on one 3-5 inch card. They hand these in to the teacher at the beginning of the session. S/he files these cards by student name. At the beginning of the end-of-course exam these cards are given to the students. Clearly those that have consistently done assigned preparation have an advantage in the exam. Note that this strategy requires very little effort on the part of the teacher; it significantly affects the amount of preparation student do for class sessions and the overall quality of work in the final exam.

- Make entry to the classroom session conditional on prior work. You will not be popular the first time you refuse entry, however, students will get the message. Clearly this strategy needs careful explaining beforehand. One example of this method was developed by Adrian Leftwich (1987, p.319) for courses in politics at York University which in part focused on issues of freedom and constraint. Students were required to write a six page critical review of assigned reading as a "ticket of admission for the seminars";

- Alternatively, accept the frequent classroom pattern where we as teachers are well prepared, but many of the students have done little prior work; the classroom sessions 'degenerate' into an impromptu lecture by the member of staff and the students pick up the 'hidden curriculum' that they need not do any preparation…

3.5 Educational theories: how do students learn?

*"You're also learning to think as well. You're exercising your brains as you go along rather than taking in the facts, maybe thinking about the facts...also processing them. **You're actually forced to.** (emphasis added)"*

(Jenkins, 1992, p.54)

All of us teach with some implicit or explicit view of how students learn and therefore how to design courses most effectively. Here I consider four influential explicit models or theories of student learning and effective course design, with examples of geographers and others who have constructed courses using these models or theories. I caution that all these theories are contested, while there are others, for example, problem-based learning (Bradbeer, 1996) which are not considered. The examples are not presented as practices we each should adopt, rather they offer us as individuals and departments, lenses through which we can view how our current courses are taught and strategies for redesigning them to make them more effective. The four perspectives considered are:

- Students learn from experience, when that experience is carefully structured.

- Teachers can design courses so that students focus on deep meaning or understanding.

- Teachers can design courses with clearly defined outcomes and assessment tasks so that students develop 'mastery' of the carefully specified content.

- Students learn effectively by constructing meaning and by linking what is taught to what they already know.

3.5.1 Teachers can design courses so that students focus on deep meaning

A powerful influence on curriculum design has been through a theory about how students approach their studies. Consider these two quotes from interviews with students. In the first one a student is describing how he reads for a particular geography course.

"I read it...trying to concentrate on what it means... There is a lot of meaning behind it. You really have to get into it and take every passage... and try to think well, what does this mean? You mustn't regurgitate what (the lecturer) is saying, that's not the idea of the exercise...it's really original ideas in this one, getting it all together."

In the second extract the interviewer has asked a student 'when you use the word learning in relation to this course what do you mean?'. He answers:

"Getting enough facts so you can write something relevant in the exam. You've got enough information so you can write an essay... I know what I've got to write without thinking about it really... I go to the next heading and regurgitate".

(Gibbs, 1992a, p.8)

Sorry its a trick! The two quotations are from the same student describing his approach to studying on two different courses. The difference in approach is not about ability, he got an upper second degree, it's about how he takes a different approach to learning in two different courses because of the way the courses are structured and the implicit and explicit messages they are giving him as to what is required.

These two quotations also illustrate two broad approaches to studying. In a surface approach the "student reduces what is to be learnt to a set of unconnected facts to be memorised; in a deep approach the student attempts to make sense of what is the learnt, which consists of ideas and concepts" (Gibbs, 1992b, p.2). Although some students find it difficult to take a deep approach, the essential point regarding course design is that students approach changes in respect to the way they perceive the course is designed. Gibbs identified those course features associated with students taking a surface approach as:

- A heavy workload (excessive demands result in students perceiving that the way to survive is to concentrate on regurgitation).

- Relatively high class contact hours.

- An excessive amount of course material.

- A lack of opportunity to study subjects in depth.

- A lack of choice over subjects and a lack of choice over the methods of study.

- A threatening and anxiety provoking assessment system.

While those features of course (and assessment) design that foster a deep approach include:

- Providing a context which **motivates** students, so that they perceive positive emotional reasons for studying the course.

- **Learner autonomy**: the course requires students to be actively constructing their learning and reflecting upon it.

- **Interaction with others**: the course design encourages or requires students to discuss their learning with others.

- **A well structured knowledge base**: not only does the student need to clearly see the structure of the courses, they also need opportunities to link that with what they already know.

There are elements of this theory which connect with others discussed here — learning from experience and constructing meaning. This theory has had considerable influence in Europe and Australia, and particularly important to the work of Biggs whose solo taxonomy has given direction to how the assessment system can promote and test deep learning (Boulton-Lewis, 1995) and Ramsden whose course experience questionnaire has been used to 'research' whether students experience their courses as promoting deep or surface learning (Wilson *et al.*, 1997).

Examples of geographers using this approach include:

- Haigh (1986), who used an earlier version of the course experience questionnaire to test the impact of an introductory physical geography course taught through 'General Systems Theory'. His preliminary conclusion was that the revised course had caused committed achievement-orientated students to search for meaning. However, less academically motivated students had become more memory-orientated in their study pattern.

- Jenkins (1992) who, in the context of a discussion of deep and surface learning in human geography, describes how over a number of years a first year course was redesigned to promote deep learning. The key changes were the move from conventional lectures to interactive discussion and workshop sessions, even though student numbers increased from c. 60-120 (see also the GDN Guide 'Lecturing in Geography' by Agnew & Elton, 1998), and radical changes in the way the course was assessed. The impact of these changes, and the way they had encouraged students to take a deep approach, was researched by interviewing students some eighteen months after they had taken the course. Here one student comments about how the workshop style lectures affected his approach. "You're also learning to think as well. You're exercising your brains as you go along rather than taking in the facts, maybe thinking about the facts…also processing them. **You're actually forced to**" (emphasis added) (Jenkins, 1992, p.54).

Individuals/departments can:

- Consider their own modules/courses through the lenses of those features described above which are seen to foster a deep or surface approach.

- Use the course experience questionnaire as a way of evaluating an individual module or a whole geography programme. Consider whether courses are promoting deep learning and what aspects might need to be changed.

3.5.2 Teachers can design courses to help students develop 'mastery'

Consider these three descriptions of courses — all of them exemplify features of 'mastery learning':

1) A first year geography course at Carleton University contains no lectures but instead "a printed study guide leads students individually through the course texts, the primary source being Peter Haggett's *Geography A Modern Synthesis*. For each unit of study, which is roughly one week's study or one chapter of the text, the guide specifies detailed learning objectives, lists the reading, poses questions and answers about the reading and provides tests for self-assessment. Students can ask questions of graduate assistants during the designated tutorial or testing sessions. When students consider themselves to be sufficiently prepared they take a short test on the whole unit, with an opportunity for review and re-testing if they fail." (Fox, *et al.*, 1987, pp.3-4; see also Fox & Wilkinson, 1977).

2) A course in spatial data analysis at the then Canberra College of Advanced Education, had students individually working their way through a practical workbook followed by a test or review exercise at the end of each unit. Should the students performance in the test be unsatisfactory the "tutor has the option of requiring the student to revise areas of weakness or undertake a second attempt at the review exercise before proceeding to the next unit" (Cho, 1982, p.136).

3)   Backler (1979, p.69) described how he had converted the traditional two lectures and one practical a week introductory course at the University of Indiana at Bloomington to one based around audio tapes and filmstrips (this was in the late 1970s). These were "available in a learning centre manned by graduate students… Students proceed through the lessons at their own pace, although they must complete a specified number of lessons before each examination."

These examples of geography courses bring out key features of 'mastery' or 'Keller'-style courses, named after the American Psychologist Keller who played a key role in developing this model of course design (Keller & Sherman, 1974). These features are:

- A clear specification of the content to be 'covered'. This may be achieved through specially written or constructed materials or through readily available materials, for example, a textbook or computer programme.

- The breaking down of that content into specific 'chunks' or units.

- The careful specification of objectives and outcomes for each unit (and the course as a whole) (Section 3.6) and the designing of assessments to test whether that has been learned.

- Regular assessments of students on what they have learned. In the 'classic' Keller form, a level of performance on that assessment is defined as mastery and students cannot proceed until they have reached that level.

- While teachers have total control over content and assessment, students have some control over when, and the pace at which, they study.

- Lectures either don't exist or are occasionally delivered either as 'reward' or to motivate and/or to orientate students to the next block of materials.

- Often graduates/students/upper-level students who have passed the course play a key role in administering the tests and giving tutorials.

Many of us have learned to type through such a programme-learned course. Their origins lie in those behavioural psychologists who in the 1960s and 1970s considered that students would learn more effectively by such tightly defined objectives. There is considerable research that demonstrates the effectiveness of these courses, particularly for certain types of material. "The technique is best suited for teaching and learning materials that are hierarchically structured and sequential, with right and wrong answers and definite criteria for testing" (Stark & Luttaca, 1997, p.221).

Such courses have been developed, particularly in the USA, for large enrolment introductory science courses. They have been seen as less appropriate to humanities and social science courses. I consider they offer one strategy for meeting the needs of increased enrolments, and diverse enrolments in large UK introductory geography courses (note that although they give the students effectively no control over what has to be learned to be assessed they do respect the fact that students with a strong background in aspects of a course can quickly demonstrate 'mastery' and move on). In the context of modular courses (Section 3.8) students will often need to spend longer on particular aspects of the introductory material to a course. Thus this approach may be appropriate to the introductory weeks to a module, enabling later weeks of the course to be taught in a more discursive open ended way, but on the basis of all students having a basic grounding in the subject. Furthermore, the more sophisticated forms of computer-based learning and assessment that are now available allow this approach to be developed without requiring the narrow reductionist model of learning from which it developed.

Things individuals/departments can do:

- Consider whether there are particular courses or sections of a module that might be appropriately taught this way.

- Conduct an experiment to try out the value of this approach. Evaluate it from both the student and staff experience and 'cost' its effectiveness (Section 3.3).

3.5.3   Teachers can design courses to help students learn from experience

Given the importance of fieldwork in geography, we can readily understand the importance of 'experiential learning': few of us would want to be operated on by a doctor who had only learned how to do it from reading a book!

The contemporary development of this approach to course design owes much to the psychologist David Kolb (1984). Essentially it argues that as individuals we have certain preferred learning styles, and that effective course design requires students to be systematically taken around all these approaches, that is to say around the experiential learning cycle (Figure 4).

Figure 4:   *The experiential learning cycle*

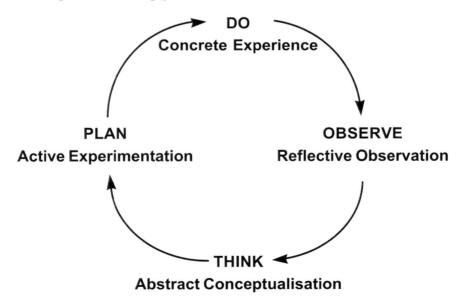

Concrete Experience:	Where the learner is actively experiencing an activity (e.g. a laboratory session, field class)
Reflective Observation:	Where the learner is consciously reflecting back on that experience
Abstract Conceptualisation:	Where the learner is being presented with/or trying to conceptualise a theory or model of what is (to be) observed
Active Experimentation:	Where the learner is trying to plan how to test a model or theory or plan for a forthcoming experience

Note that the theory does not imply that experience by itself is enough or most important; indeed without the other stages little may be learned; nor does it say that courses should start with students experiencing something. One can design the course to start at any stage of the learning cycle. What is important is to systematically take the learner around each stage, ensuring that effective links are being made between each stage. This model does offer an explicit critique of those laboratory courses or fieldwork programmes that are not explicitly linked to the more theoretical and often lecture-based elements of the course. It is similarly critical of those higher experiential activities (for example, certain field courses, simulations and games) where students receive little preparation for the experience and more fundamentally no effective chance to reflect upon the experience and relate it to their wider reading. Thus, effective use of simulations in courses can benefit considerably from both teachers and students being aware of and using this approach.

While one may choose a course or an activity to take students just once around the cycle, in its fuller form one designs the course to systematically take them through the cycle a number of times, as is explained in the following example of a field course. The stage of cycle, for example, Abstract Conceptualisation (AC) is first set in brackets.

Using the experiential learning cycle to teach a field course

Before the field course:

Stage 1 (AC):   Students required to do reading on competing theories on the geography of post-industrial societies.

Stage 2 (AE):   In project groups, students plan questions to test these models, with defined interest groups and set up interviews for opening days of the field course.

On the field course:

Stage 3 (CE):   Initial interviews.

Stage 4 (RO):   Structured discussion or journal writing which gets student to reflect.

Stage 5 (AC):   Tentative statement about validity of models as applied to this location/interest group.

Stage 6 (AE):   Planning questions to further test revised model in subsequent interview.

Stage 7 (CE):   Further interviews.

The cycle can be maintained but at some point (probably at AC or AE) there is closure.

3.5.4   Teachers can design courses to help students construct meaning

In the educational video '*A Private Universe*' (Pyramid Films, California) we see students graduating from Harvard University. We then see individual students being interviewed and asked to explain the causes of the seasons. Many of their answers reveal a pre-Copernican understanding of the universe. Yet we then hear how many of them have taken and passed advanced courses in environmental science and astronomy.

One way of explaining this apparent dysfunction between students formal accredited knowledge and the misconceptions of their everyday knowledge is that their courses have failed to help them connect the two and therefore change their everyday understanding to a post-Copernican universe. They still think within their 'private universe'.

This 'case study' serves as a brief introduction to the idea or principle that students learn by constructing meaning. As we get into this literature (see in particular Laurillard, 1993) we come across terms such as 'situated cognition' and 'phenomenography'! Put simply this broad approach sees course design not as "a process of dumping information into the empty brains of the students. Rather, teaching involves figuring out what learners already know (including misconceptions about a given subject), building upon that existing knowledge and helping learners make connections between new information and prior learning so that they can understand and retain the new material" (Cross & Steadman, 1996, p.37).

Laurillard (1993, p.28) puts it in a slightly different way: "Teaching is essentially a rhetorical activity, seeking to persuade students to change the way that they experience the world. It has to create the environment that will enable students to learn the descriptions of the world devised by others". To Laurillard (1997, p.172) that is why small group discussion is so important in the traditional university context, because there "through debate and discussion with the teacher…the student can begin to see how the specialist language works, how the **discourse proceeds in a particular discipline**" (emphasis added). That is why effective curriculum design gives students opportunities to continually reshape, through discussion, their understanding of the world, and through course structures which require them to reshape that understanding through the ideas and the specialist language of disciplinary enquiry. Such discussions in some institutions, like Harvard University, may still be in small university seminars. However, it is more likely to be found in courses where traditional lectures have been replaced by interactive lectures or workshops (Jenkins 1992; Agnew & Elton, 1997) or as Laurillard (1993; 1997), who is pro-Vice Chancellor at the Open University, demonstrates through the interactive information technology of the 1990s.

Examples of courses taking this approach include:

- An Open University introductory Art History course, which starts from the recognition that there is likely to be an initial mismatch between students and staff perception of the discipline. "Academics see the subject as highly theoretical…", students may well "come to the subject because they want to know more about paintings…for the students in many courses the immersion in theory occurs before they feel grounded in the experience of the phenomena being described" (Laurillard, 1997, pp.177-8). An initial activity gets students to sort, using a computer programme, some 20 pictures into categories that make sense to them, using and developing their everyday language. The programme then gradually introduces them to the way and the language that certain art historians would explain and categorise these paintings.

- Hounsell (1997), who describes how those constructing an Open University course on the Third World interviewed perspective students for their understanding of terms such as 'developed' and 'Third World'. This gave the course team a clear sense of the audience they were addressing in constructing the course. Also, an initial exercise had students analysing their own preconceptions, while later course work assignment had them carrying out an investigation of a sample group of the general public to ascertain their perceptions of the Third World and relate that to the academic perceptions they had encountered in the course. Harrison (1995) from the Cheltenham & Gloucester College of Higher Education describes how, in a geography module on 'Images of the Third World', she gets students to juxtapose their own academic understanding of the third world developed through the course with those in the popular media (http://www.chelt.ac.uk/gdn/abstracts/a12.htm).

The above examples clearly indicate how those cultural and social geographers interested in issues of representation can use this approach in developing their courses. However, these examples may have given the perception that his approach is less suited to the more 'objective' world of physical geography. Let us return to those Harvard University graduates. These were students who at one level had 'mastered' the objective knowledge in the course. But what may have been missing in these courses were opportunities for them to articulate their prior conceptions of these phenomena, to continually interrogate and reformulate these perceptions as they learnt the formal academic discourse and knowledge that also explained these phenomena. Laurillard (1993; 1997) provides examples of how students understanding of rainfall, geological mapping, ecology…can be developed through curricula that recognise that what students bring to learning and how they construct their meaning needs to be central to course design.

3.6 Aims and objectives

'If students don't know where you are heading, how can they know they are on the right track or what they can expect on arrival?'.

"She said hey, do you know where you're coming from? ***Hey, do you know where you're going to?***"

(from the song "Do you know where you're coming from?" [emphasis added] Jamiroquai, from the album "Travelling Without Moving", 1996)

Many of us are aware of aims and objectives, and they are increasingly required by some universities. In the UK, the TQA methodology and now the QAA methodology, by judging quality against objectives, encourages departments to express, if only on paper, a set of aims and objectives for their course. Thus there are clearly political reasons (Section 1.4) for expressing our curricula in the language of aims and objectives. Here our focus is the educational reasons and values in using this approach. To appreciate its power consider these questions:

For an individual module or course you teach and/or for the geography programme in which you are centrally involved:

- Think of the students at the beginning of the course. What has geography as a discipline to contribute that is potentially so valuable to them?

- Picture those same students at the end of the module/geography programme. **What do you want them to be able to know and do** as a result of taking that module/programme? Write that in a way that clearly expresses your thoughts. Write that in a way that is clear to someone else, for example, a student on the course, a colleague or an employer.

- Think of yourself as someone who on graduation might hire that student as an employee, or as a researcher, what **evidence** could students produce that they have satisfactorily achieved these objectives?

These questions have hopefully indicated the nature and power of the approach of designing a course through aims and objectives. Using the language of 'aims and objectives' can be a linguistic hoop that we jump through to meet external quality requirements. However, if we colonise and use that language it can be a powerful tool to improve our curricula for ourselves and our students.

3.6.1 Defining aims and objectives

Aims are long-term goals which are often related to political and philosophical perspectives on the nature of geography, for example, 'students will obtain: an awareness of the inter-relation between physical and human processes; an understanding of the role of the physical processes in shaping the earth's surface; an appreciation of the particularities of place'. These are important value statements and express the direction we want students to take. For students, they give a sense of whether the course will meet their interests and goals. Their limitation is that they lack precision, for example what is meant by 'understanding'? How would a student know she had got there? Objectives and learning outcomes enable us to define more precisely what we mean by such aims and to be sure whether students have got there. The difference is indicated in the box below:

In stating our aims we use words like:	In stating our objectives or outcomes we use words like:
know	list
understand	describe
be familiar with	evaluate
become acquainted with	state
have a good grasp of	explain
obtain a working knowledge of	select

Some institutions prefer, or even require, the phrase 'learning outcome' in their documentation. The distinction is not just semantic: the word 'objective' specifies the direction we want the student to take; expressing that as an 'outcome' enables us and the students to know whether they have got there. For example, the aims of a course on the geography of China might be 'to appreciate how Western values shape the reality of China that is perceived'. The outcomes might include: 'at the end of the module you will be able to:

- identify how western geography texts written in the period 1850-1997 reflect the then immediate geopolitical preoccupations of the western powers;

- analyse how the changing geography of China that is perceived in these texts reflects the changing geopolitical preoccupations of the Western powers.'

A piece of course work testing whether the students had achieved the first outcome might be:

'Below are short extracts from 3 British geography texts on the geography of China written in 1867, 1951 and 1997. Write a 1500-word article for the sixth-form journal *Geography Review* that identifies how these extracts reveal contemporary British geopolitical preoccupations, and present the argument that readers of this journal should not expect writings on the geography of China, or elsewhere, to be *objective*.'

Note how the verbs in learning outcomes are 'active' verbs: they direct us as to what students should do, while the verbs used in aims are relatively 'passive'. Learning outcomes also help us with our concern with the academic level we want students to achieve. Here the work of Bloom (1956) and others in the USA has been very influential in defining six levels of cognitive activity: they demonstrate a hierarchy of levels with knowledge as the lowest level and each level building on the other. The six levels, with some of their associated active learning outcome verbs, are:

Level 1 — Knowledge
Possible verbs: define, distinguish, identify, list, recognise, describe, draw

Level 2 — Comprehension
Possible verbs: translate, transform, illustrate, express in your own words, represent, change, rephrase, restate, explain, interpret, sort, rearrange, differentiate, distinguish, demonstrate, estimate, infer, conclude, predict, fill in, extend, determine, interpolate, extrapolate

Level 3 — Application
Possible verbs: apply, generalise, relate, choose, develop, organise, use, employ, transfer, classify

Level 4 — Analysis
Possible verbs: analyse, distinguish, detect, deduce, classify, discriminate, recognise, categorise, compare

Level 5 — Synthesis
Possible verbs: write, relate, produce, construct, draw, originate, modify, document, design, plan, specify, derive, combine, synthesise, develop

Level 6 — Evaluation

Possible verbs: judge, argue, validate, evaluate, assess, decide, select, compare, appraise, discuss

We can use this list, which is not exhaustive, to write learning outcomes for our modules and to create appropriate assessment tasks. There is not a simple one-to-one relation between verb and programme level. However, if most of the verbs in an advanced module are from level one it is possible students are not being required to work at a high enough level. What is more likely is that we are expecting students to work at a high level, and are probably assessing them at that level, but the way we describe our course does not make that clear to them. Expressing it clearly in that way can help us and them to achieve that level. Rowntree (1981) who has considerably influenced the move in the UK to an objectives-based approach summarises the advantages as:

- enabling teachers to communicate their intentions more clearly to colleagues and students;

- enabling staff in a department to discuss productively what they want to achieve;

- providing a framework for the selection of course content, appropriate teaching methods and forms of assessment.

Is a syllabus still required?

Yes! A syllabus setting out the content, the topics to be covered, reading to be done, the assessment tasks and perhaps a weekly schedule also provides students and colleagues with a map of the course. The learning outcomes provide students with a statement of what they should be able to do with that syllabus when they get to the end of this journey.

3.6.2 Limitations and extensions

There are limitations to an objectives/outcomes approach to curriculum design. At its extreme it can be too reductionist and ignore the unexpected or unintended outcomes of a course. This can be dealt with by activities and assessments which get students at the end of the course to consider the intended outcomes and then to use that language to express what they consider they have achieved. The reductionist element in it can, in part, be covered by specifying outcomes not just at the level of individual modules but also specifying them for a whole programme or degree course (see below).

Perhaps also the value to teachers of objectives/outcomes has not been helped by them being seen by some educationists and 'quality' agencies as the place we have to start (and certainly when setting out our QAA statement).

This ignores the fact that most of us are likely to start elsewhere, for example, from our research interests or increasingly from how much time we can afford. That is why I suggest the ouija board model as a framework for curriculum design, for we can start anywhere but consider all factors; and then prioritise what we consider appropriate. Rowntree (1981, p.35) states that he moved away from decreeing that one should start with objectives because he came "to realise that my course planning does not necessarily begin with objectives... However this certainly does not mean I am renouncing objectives."

Things a department can do:

- Require all modules to be set out using the language of learning outcomes.

- Agree on a list of graduate learning outcomes, for example, a clear statement of what all students who graduate from a geography programme/degree course should be able to do. Some UK institutions, for example, Oxford Brookes, Liverpool John Moores and Thames Valley Universities are requiring all course teams to do that. At Oxford Brookes University it is called a graduate profile.

- Research the views of graduating students (Section 3.10) as to what they consider they know and can do as a result of studying geography and compare it with staff perceptions; this may lead us to change our graduate profile.

- Review the overall assessment of the geography programme and consider whether it effectively supports students in achieving those outcomes (Section 3.7).

- Decide on whether certain outcomes are required to be passed or achieved before moving on to the next level or to graduate from the geography programme.

- In a final synoptic module, require students to write a statement of the outcomes they consider they have achieved; this does not necessarily have to be an assessed activity. It is also an activity that can aid them when applying for jobs.

Things an individual lecturer can do:

- Describe their module in terms of learning outcomes and ensure that the assessment supports students in achieving them.

- Design an activity for the beginning of the module which gets students to consider the learning outcomes and express them in a language that makes sense to them. Also, get them to identify the outcome they most wish to develop, perhaps including some you have not specified.

- Halfway through the module get students to consider which of these outcomes they are achieving and those they now need to concentrate upon or need staff support with.

- At the end of the module get students to review their learning and evaluate the module against the outcomes determined at the beginning of the module.

3.7 Assessment as learning: a department assessment strategy

*"There is a growing diversity of assessment methods… Nevertheless, in about 30 per cent of departments the assessors considered the assessment regime to be too dependent upon unseen examinations and essays… **Best practice occurs where there is a close match between the intended learning outcomes and the assessment methods used.**"*

(HEFCE, 1995a, p.9). Emphasis added.

"A multiform (department) assessment system...recognises that after leaving university a person must work sometimes under great pressure, sometimes alone, sometimes in a team, sometimes relying on memory, and sometimes with all the freedom of time, reflection and advice from others."

(King, 1976, p.231)

Closely linked to an emphasis on designing through course objectives/outcomes (Section 3.6), is an approach to curriculum design which sees assessment as central to the curriculum students experience, and which should be central to the curriculum which staff design.

This is sometimes contrasted with a stereotyped staff curriculum design process where individual staff first think of the content to be taught, decide how to divide that up in the weeks to be taught...and then much later decide what essay questions/objective tests to set. As staff work on these assessment decisions individually, students in a programme or course experience a set of unco-ordinated assessment decisions. Clearly this is an exaggerated picture but I think this a valid critique.

There are three key reasons why assessment should be central to curriculum design:

- Educationally there is strong research evidence that assessment profoundly shapes the hidden curriculum that student's experience. Students to varying extents pick out from the assessment process what staff value. As Peter Gould (1973, p.260) argued in *The Open Geographic Curriculum*: "Learning large quantities of fact and being required to regurgitate them by multiple choice questions (USA) or by waffle ignorance-cloaking essays (Europe) is not going to help students tomorrow." To which I would add: but it will immediately determine the curriculum they pay attention to, and this will determine what they take forward into their lives. There is also growing evidence that as students do paid work outside college they are much more selective in relation to their college work and focus exclusively on what will be (immediately) assessed (for example, Sacks, 1996). So educationally a key curriculum decision is the assessment tasks we set.

- Internationally, there are moves that focus the quality assurance of teaching on assessment and particularly on the standards, or the 'competencies ' of graduating students. Here the focus of concern is at the level of a course team and the institution. By the time this booklet is read, UK geographers will no doubt be familiar with the QAA process and its (likely) focus on threshold standards and subject-based benchmarks (see Section 1.4). There are very similar trends in the USA where the regional accreditation authorities (for example, the North Central Association) are requiring institutions and departments to have assessment strategies and evidence of the abilities and knowledge of graduating students. Indeed, many States are mandating graduate assessment strategies and evidence of student accomplishment as a condition of State financial support. Politically, I think such requirements will become internationally required. We may not like that. However, we should recognise that as a department we need an assessment strategy if only on paper!

- For our own health and to ensure we have time to do other things (such as research), as a department we need an assessment strategy. The international pressures of having to do more with less, of having to teach larger classes at higher student-staff ratios requires a fundamental re-think of course design (see Section 3.3). This should include a major re-design by a department of its assessment strategy. Otherwise the load of assessing more students can cause considerable strain to staff and threaten their health. The assessment load on staff can also threaten the time available for research. Yet the evidence from UK geography departments is that, while by the early 1990s while many had changes to their teaching methods to cope with budget cuts and teaching at higher SSRs, few had then made such changes in their methods of assessment. (Jenkins & Smith, 1993). Some have now made key changes — for example, the use of computer aided assessment at Aberdeen (Chapman, 1997) and Leeds and in UK geography departments the widespread use of assessed group work (for example, Burkill, 1997). However I think that in many departments more widespread and strategic changes need to be made. Indeed there is anecdotal evidence and limited research evidence, that recently in some institutions there has been a set of individual staff decisions to cut expensive forms of assessment such as coursework essays. This may well have resulted in students spending very little time doing academic work, and staff complaining about this and the threat to academic standards. There are things that individual staff can do with respect to the assessment of their own courses (Gibbs, 1992d). However for significant change that protects staff time, while ensuring the quality of student learning, there needs to be collective action at a departmental level (and ideally at institutional and regional/national levels).

For reasons explained above my focus is on department and/or programme strategies. I do not consider what individual staff can do — though that hopefully is implicit. Nor do I consider the vital question of the choice and design of particular assessment methods. A related Guide in this series *Assessment in Geography* (Bradford & O'Connell, 1998) gives advice and examples on a range of assessment methods. These include both the traditional (UK) essay exams, and how to involve students in assessing their work and that of their peers; how to design group-based assessments and (computer marked) objective tests. In addition there is suggestions on a range of departmental level issues including matching outcomes and assessment, reliable marking and degree classification. So there is much in that Guide that complements this section.

3.7.1   Codifying and developing current practice

In developing our department strategy we will find that there is limited public experience to draw upon and few published accounts. For example, in over 20 years there is but one article in the *Journal of Geography in Higher Education* that analyses a department assessment strategy (Goodall, 1977). In geography Russell King (1976) undertook the one major study of department assessment practises but that was from the early 1970s on the then UK University sector. As the international focus on assessment gathers pace we should have more published accounts to draw upon.

However, despite the dearth of published guidance, as a department we have our own past experience and practice to draw on. In certain cases developing an assessment strategy may simply mean codifying and developing what is our current practice. In many other cases, however, I think it will require a fundamental re-design, and what follows are suggestions on doing that. In the rest of this section I offer suggestions on how as a department, one can approach curriculum design through developing an assessment strategy.

- I start by first looking at Alverno's institution-wide strategy. Alverno is internationally recognised as the leader in this approach to curriculum design.

- I then turn too more limited specific suggestions that departments could adapt and integrate into their current policy. In particular I show how one can try to ensure that the assessment methods support the overall programme objectives; describe methods that enable a department to map and review the methods currently used and then use this as a springboard for re-designing the assessment curriculum; and indicate ways to be rigorous about graduate threshold outcomes and standards.

- I conclude by suggesting how this focus on assessment can be achieved while recognising the need to limit staff workloads.

3.7.2 A preface to the description of Alverno

In considering the analysis of Alverno below, you can choose to argue why you could not adopt their practice. However I hope you and I will focus on how you could *adapt* their practice to your very different (national) institutional and department contexts. The details of the approach do reflect very particular circumstances: a liberal arts institution with a focus on undergraduate teaching, relatively small class sizes, and what may be most significant — a long-term focused institutional leadership. For these changes have taken some twenty five years to develop and embed. However, I argue that if one focuses on the general principles of the approach then the ideas and practices could be selectively adapted to your department.

Alverno College (Milwaukee) (http://www.alverno.edu/) is a small women's college that from the early 1970s has developed an innovative curriculum focused around an integration of the disciplines and the abilities. There are a set of College agreed abilities that all disciplines have to develop and assess (problem solving, communication, aesthetic responsiveness, effective citizenship…), and each one of these abilities is defined at a range of levels. Geography is not one of the disciplines studied. This curriculum clearly has echoes of the moves in the UK and elsewhere to require/encourage the development of transferable/life skills (see the Guide in this series by Chalkley & Harwood, 1998, and the case study in this Guide of Oxford Brookes University, Section 4.3).

What is also distinctive about the Alverno curriculum and immediately relevant here is the focus of the Alverno curriculum on 'assessment as learning' (Alverno College Faculty, 1994). Students graduate with a faculty narrative statement of the student's *performance* of the Alverno abilities in the disciplines studied. The curriculum focus on assessment is on helping individual students to develop and be aware of their abilities in the context of the disciplines they have studied. Over twenty five years much staff time has been devoted to defining the key abilities that students are required to develop (for example, problem solving), to specifying what that ability means at six specified levels, and in discussing in the various disciplines how these abilities can best be developed. For each ability there is a carefully defined set of criteria for student performance. The boxed section sets out what I see are some of the general principles of the approach. Before you consider the general principles, it may help to consider two-assessment exercises all students undertake whatever their discipline. In their first semester all students visit the college assessment centre where they will:

- Have a speech videoed. Using the criteria for the communication ability, a member of staff will help the student assess her own performance and guide her on how to improve. A copy of the video will be centrally stored and at various stages of her studies the student will have other speeches videoed, and, by both self and staff assessment, analyse and record how her performance in this communication ability is developing.

- During her first semester each student will take part in a group problem solving exercise with some 5-6 students. During the exercise each student's 'performance' will be assessed by a trained external assessor. (These are unpaid people from business, public service agencies, and so on, who are rigorously trained in assessing the abilities and giving feedback.) After the exercise is completed each individual student will receive detailed feedback on how she had performed in the problem solving and social interaction ability.

Though these centrally organised assessments dramatise the institutional approach, the emphasis of the overall curriculum is in staff devising related curricula and assessments *in the disciplines* that support students in developing the ability. The approach is described below.

Benefiting from Alverno's approach to curriculum design through assessment

You can adapt Alverno's philosophy of 'assessment as learning' by as a department (and as an individual) asking these questions:

In our discipline/course

- Which College-defined/department-defined abilities can students develop? Or what do we expect/require students from this geography programme to be able to know and do?

- What performances/forms of assessment would demonstrate that students have achieved this ability as applied in my discipline to the required level? (i.e. the curriculum is virtually starting from assessment design.)

- How does this proposed assessment meet the professional judgement of my peers in my discipline — particularly in terms of how it will demonstrate the students performance in this ability? (At Alverno, staff in the disciplines and in cross-institutional teams regularly meet to discuss issues of assessment.)

- How can we support the students to reach this level of performance in this assessment context? This will include curricula decisions about the selection and organisation of content — but at Alverno this is a much later decision than the usual curriculum design process.

- How can we give feedback/formative assessment to students during the course?

- How can students assess their developing performance during this course?

- How can this process of self assessment in my course/our discipline help this individual student to reflect on her development as a learner with respect to the 'abilities' we have defined for this institution/ department?

- How can we help this student in developing these abilities in our discipline to transfer her abilities to the other courses she will learn and to her life (including employment) when she graduates?

- What form of evidence should the student and the College record to give external evidence (including to an employer) of student performance in the abilities.

- What is the research evidence as to the impact of our discipline in developing student abilities after they have graduated? (*c.* 3% of the Alverno institutional budget is devoted to rigorous research on the long-term impact of the curriculum. Note how this compares with the UK practice of just considering the employment statistics 6 months after graduation, and think how much of your department's research budget is spent on the impact of the curriculum!)

- In the light of this research evidence how should we in our discipline re-design how students are assessed?

Adapting Alverno to a department's assessment strategy

In my view (drawing on extensive discussions with Alverno staff), we can take the central elements of their culture and selectively adapt it. Here is how I think a geography department could use Alverno to shape it's assessment strategy. (For fuller analyses of the Alverno curriculum and how it might be adapted to other contexts see Gibbs, 1994a, and the analyses of and discussion with Alverno staff on the Web pages of the Ability Based Network http://www.brookes.ac.uk/services/ocsd/abchome.html.)

As a department/programme

- Start by defining a profile of the abilities/knowledge you would expect graduate students to achieve (see Section 3.6 and in particular the boxed description describing an individual module or course that you teach). Such graduate profiles are now being required/encouraged in a number of UK and US institutions and in the case of Oxford Brookes University was directly based on the Alverno model. While the Oxford Brookes experience shaped the QAA decision to require that in their (draft) requirements (see Figure 1) departments are required to state "what a graduate should know and be able to do on completion of the programme."

- Having specified your graduate outcomes, now specify the types of evidence/forms of assessment that will enable students to demonstrate that they have acquired that knowledge and/or developed those abilities.

  This close coupling at a programme level between programme outcomes and assessment methods is for me a key lesson to take from Alverno and one that is applicable to all programmes. (Albeit in certain programmes where students have considerable choice this will have to be more loosely developed.)

- For each type of assessment specify the criteria that would demonstrate that a student had reached the levels of performance assessment used in your national system/department. For example, how would you collectively determine a student's research dissertation was first class? (This should bring out that in many cases departments already have elements of this approach.)

- As a department, and perhaps involving the external examiner or a respected geographer from another institution, review how different staff are assessing these final assessments. Use this to draw up a common understanding with clearly stated criteria for performance levels on graduation.

- Ensure that the balance and range of assessment methods used reflect your (stated) values and programme objectives. At Alverno, there is a strong focus on assessment exercises that require individual students to make moral judgements and to assess their own performance in that ability. In geography departments which aim to develop students' ability to do independent research (see Section 3.2 and the case study of University College London in Section 4.2), there should be a range and progression of assessments that develop that ability.

- Rigorously research/evaluate whether the forms of evidence and types of knowledge that students take forward to employers (postgraduate courses) actually help the students to present what they have learned and the employers to judge their potential (see Section 3.10).

- Rigorously research/evaluate whether students are clearly aware of the (implicit) assessments, that are used in the course, and the values they represent.

- On the basis of the above re-design the graduating assessments.

- Then consider the forms of assessment used throughout the programme. How do they support students in developing the qualities that will enable them to perform in the graduating assessments?

- Now go back 'down' the curriculum and at some point focus on induction. How can we design the student experience to ensure they are aware of the assessment values and practices in this department? Consider again those two exercises all Alverno students undertake. What could we do in our department that adapts that initial emphasis on assessment to our own course structures and values?

I see this approach to assessment design as applying to very different contexts than Alverno. However, I well recognise that at first reading, it may seem far too radical, and/or inappropriate to your context. Nevertheless you will note elements of it in the more specific methods outlined below — all of which can be developed by an individual department.

3.7.3   Link programme graduate outcomes to department assessment practices

"Best practice occurs where there is a close match between the intended learning outcomes and the assessment methods used."

(HEFCE, 1995a, p.9)

The principle of linking programme outcomes to assessment practices, has already been mentioned both in the above discussion of adapting Alverno and in the prior discussion of aims and objectives (Section 3.6). Here the main elements of this approach will be restated and certain problems in implementation discussed.

- As a department one starts by agreeing the central knowledge, skills and attributes that distinguish a graduate from this department.

- One then considers how the assessment process can be best developed to develop those attributes/outcomes. Here you need some agreement of the strengths of different forms of assessment and indeed a typology of the different assessment methods used in the department. The one outlined below can provide a starting point.

Table 2: *Assessment practices for different objectives/outcomes*

Objective/Outcome	Appropriate assessment
Memorisation of factual knowledge of geography	Objective tests; unseen examinations
Comprehension of key specific concepts and principles	Short essay questions including unseen exams; objective tests that are designed to test at this level
Practical skills	Laboratory exercises; fieldwork assessments etc.
Independence ,creativity and problem solving	Longer essays where student has greater choice over topic and form of writing
	Laboratory/field exercise where both problem and method of analysis only initially outlined by staff
	Dissertation/project with (limited) staff supervision
Integration of ideas and knowledge	Longer essays where student has full access to library etc.
Groupwork	Assessed exercises where student is assessed as a member of the group
Oral and presentation skills	Spoken presentations, vivas, assessed games and simulations

(based on King, 1976)

- Table 2 is presented as a beginning typology. What is important is for you to discuss and agree an assessment typology you consider appropriate.

- One then reviews the match (or perhaps mismatch) between the programme outcomes and methods of assessment. This might lead to changes in the assessment methods or to the outcomes — that is to say, you may decide that you think the assessment is appropriate — but it is supporting a different outcome than you originally formulated.

One of the problems in implementing this approach is getting collective department agreement on assessment. The issue of achieving collective departmental agreement is one that implicitly runs through this entire Guide and is considered in the conclusion (Section 5). Collective agreement on an assessment strategy could be sought at a department level through a workshop, or it could be more inductively achieved by someone analysing the individual module descriptions and from that proposing a collective framework.

Clearly this ' tight coupling' between programme outcomes and methods of assessment could have been better achieved in the traditional UK linear degree programme. In modular programmes that are now internationally the norm (Section 3.9) more modest coupling should be sought. What I do not think is acceptable is to leave the linkage as proposed in the draft QAA framework (Figure 1). That only requires "assessment criteria linked to learning outcomes for each module," and assumes that simply adding the assessment criteria for a set of individual modules will amount to a coherent whole. It also fails to ensure that key knowledge and skills are given central consideration in the programme assessment. While for internal or external reviewers the level of detailed analysis required by considering each individual module means that the overall assessment curriculum is unlikely to be perceived. Hopefully — well from my values — the revised QAA specification will require a tighter coupling than just the linkage at module level. Also, to anticipate one of the themes of a forthcoming discussion (Section 3.9), modular courses can be designed to ensure such assessment coherence but this again requires collective department action.

Things a department can do:

If you agree with this analysis and want to ensure a modest coupling between assessment and module outcomes, you might decide to create a strategy to link outcomes and assessment (Figure 5):

- Ensure that in core compulsory courses/modules there is both a close match and coherent pattern of assessment methods.

- Ensure that in those core courses there is a range of assessment methods that supports students to develop the key disciplinary knowledge and transferable skills you consider appropriate and have stated in your programme specification.

- Concentrate on those modules/courses that are central to final degree classification or honours classification.

- In programmes with considerable student choice you could target the assessment pattern for those modules that are a major consistent element of student choice.

Figure 5: *A strategy to link graduate/programme outcomes and assessment (after Jackson, 1998)*

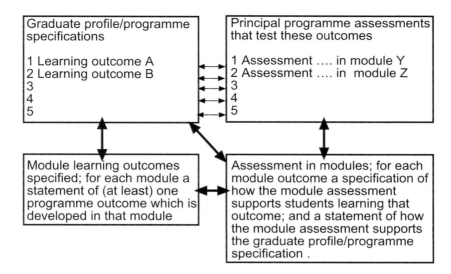

- Give staff considerable freedom over most of the outcomes and methods of assessment for individual modules, but require them to specify for each of their modules how the assessment centrally supports one graduate/programme outcome.

- Requiring staff to state clearly that linkage in the description of the course given to students could further ensure the linkage at a module and programme level.

- Ensure that there is an evaluation or research strategy (Section 3.10) that analyses the effectiveness of this linkage.

In all these approaches to the coupling of assessment and outcomes, the idea of mapping assessment practices is a useful tool.

3.7.4   Mapping and auditing department assessment practices

As geographers we are well aware of the strengths and limitations of maps and diagrams. They both reveal and distort a complex reality. Recognising that they provide both a powerful and limited picture enables us to use them effectively.

The approach is demonstrated by a review of the geography programme at Jacksonville State (Johnson, 1995) (Figure 6).

Figure 6: *Sample matrix of courses required for geography major students (after Johnson, 1995)*

COURSE#/TITLE									STANDARDS										SKILLS				
	1	2	3	4	5	6	7	8	9	10	11	12	13	14	15	16	17	18	1	2	3	4	5
208- Map Reading	**		**		**														**	**	**	**	
220- Cultural Geography		**	**	**	**				**	**	**	**	**	**	**	**		**					
240- Physical Geography			**	**			**	**						**	**	**			**			**	**
245- Physical Lab		**					**	**											**	**	**	**	**
307- Geog. Info Sys	**		**						**	**	**	**		**					**	**	**	**	**
315- Research Methods	**		**																**	**	**	**	**
490- Colloquium																							

The department wished to review its range of courses to see whether they enabled students to meet the goals of the National Geography Standards. This is a national statement of the goals of geography that should be apparent in all programmes, for example, 'the use of maps...to report information from a spatial perspective'. Originally developed for pre-college courses the department decided to use it to review its programme. Here it is the idea of mapping assessment (and course content) that is considered, not the idea of 'Geography Standards'. Figure 6 shows where the particular standards and skills were clearly apparent in the assessment of courses which were required for a geography major student. As Johnson (*ibid*, p.536) argues information organised in this fashion facilitates discussion... It allows you to discuss specifics rather than just talk in general terms. Together (as a department) you can see exactly what is, and is not being covered." Figure 7 sets out one other way of mapping or auditing the pattern of assessment used in a programme.

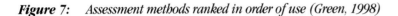

***Figure* 7:**   *Assessment methods ranked in order of use (Green, 1998)*

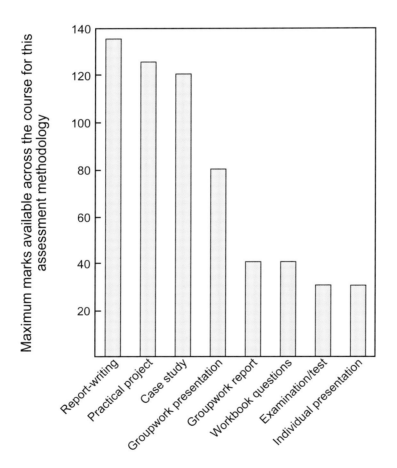

The idea of mapping assessment is essentially the same as the idea of mapping transferable skills (and their assessment), as shown in Figure 9 (Section 4.3.4). One needs to make a careful decision on what information you want to map and to what purpose. There is no one way to map or diagram the assessment in a programme. Indeed, it is probably important over a period of years to use a range of maps or audit tools that will reveal different assessment realities. Clear initial definitions are important. Thus you are certain to need an agreed typology of assessment methods. You will need a norm or level at which the assessment is considered significant enough to count/map. Therefore, you could agree to 'only record when the assessment method counts for at least twenty five percent of the course grade.' The assessment map can then reveal much to a department (and to students and review panels) about the curriculum. For example, Figure 7 tells us much about the effective curriculum that those students experience. It reveals a very different reality than the traditional listing of course content or the more recent statement of course objectives.

Doing this or a related audit for your department enables you to have an informed discussion of whether and how your assessment strategy needs revising. It also dramatises the explicit argument of this section of the Guide that *assessment is a central element of the curriculum*.

3.7.5   Be rigorous about graduate assessment requirements and threshold standards

"Academic standards (are)...explicit levels of academic attainment that are used to describe and measure academic requirements and achievements of individual students and groups of students... Student assessment is clearly central to standards. If the work of students is not assessed by valid and reliable methods, standards cannot be rigorous."

(Higher Education Quality Council, 1997c, pp.5 & 8)

"Analysis of degree results in geography in United Kingdom universities between 1973-90 reveals persistent and systematic variations between departments in the proportion of good degrees awarded."

(Chapman, 1994, p.89).

Though the above two quotations are from the immediate UK context, they illustrate an international move to require more explicit statements from universities about what graduating students know and can do (see Section 1.4). Chapman's work can also be seen as part of a concern within the academic community itself about the standards students are achieving in the context of the massification of higher education. In short, somewhat different drivers (for example, the external environment and our own professional concerns) push us to a more explicit focus on the standards of geography graduates.

I think that for those of us in the UK this is central to the political context in which we will be working in the next few years. Our colleagues in the USA are already there. For example, in 1979 the geography department in Knoxville Tennessee introduced a special graduating assessment examination as Tennessee State funding effectively mandated such programme assessment (Jumper, 1992). By 1997 three quarters of US states had legislated some form of graduating assessment requirements as a condition of state funding.

Things a department can do:

- Follow Chapman (1994; 1996) and statistically analyse the pattern of marks of students in the geography programme and compare it to the pattern in previous years and to that in other comparable departments.

- Learn from the wide and varied good practice US good practice in a range of disciplines (Banta *et al.*, 1996). Note though, that in some cases this involves extra assessments of students outside their courses. To limit our own workloads we should all seek to ensure that key in-course assessments are valid and reliable. Ensure that those assessments that are the central requirements for honours and/or whose marks constitute most of the final student degree result are assessed in ways that are valid and reliable. In most UK geography departments this will focus our attention on the ways we assess the dissertation. See the case study below.

David Pepper of the geography department at Brookes (with a sociology colleague), carried out an action research study (see Section 3.10) of dissertation marking at Brookes in a range of disciplines including geography (Pepper & Webster, 1998). This included an analysis by an independent researcher of the reports by geography staff explaining the grade they awarded. One of the central research questions was the extent to which the assessors were using pre–agreed and supposedly common assessment criteria, or to what extent were other implicit criteria being used. The possible actions to take in the light of this research are 'now' under discussion. That discussion is in part focusing on the practicality and desirability of common assessment criteria — see below.

- Consider developing similar exercises to that at Oxford Brookes University in your department. Doing this puts you into contested territory. Not only are you opening up to scrutiny issues, which are personally sensitive, but it is also a contentious issue in the educational literature. Put crudely, the tensions and the academic disputes are between those who argue for professional autonomy and those who emphasise the need for public accountability; and between those who see the need for explicit criteria and performance standards in assessment and those who see assessment as akin to wine tasting — a high level activity that requires continued practice but that is impenetrable to outsiders (de Vries, 1996; Wright, 1996). As a department I suspect you are going to have to make your view on this issue explicit and be able to justify it to outsiders (including internal review panels). Those who favour the wine tasting 'connoisseur' model of assessment will probably need to ensure that there are regular procedures for discussion amongst staff of implicit criteria, and activities in the curriculum that make students aware of the underlying staff/disciplinary values that shape how they are assessed. You will certainly need to present on paper why you think this approach is justified. Those in the other 'camp' are likely to develop explicit and agreed (and monitored) assessment criteria, which are clearly documented and explained to students — like Alverno! Whichever route you choose, you are shaping the curriculum students will experience.

- In the UK we should recognise that the external examiner system gives us one key source for verifying standards. You may choose to negotiate with the external to help the department (annually) target the review of particular assessments — for example, do the assessments of core courses show definite levels of complexity of tasks set?

- Consider benchmarking your methods and levels of assessment with a comparable department. In the UK there are pressures for the discipline to agree common benchmark standards across a discipline (QAA, 1998). Many perceive that attempting to set up common national standards for say a first-class degree in geography would both stifle diversity and is attempting the impossible. What is certainly far more feasible is for institutions with a common philosophy and 'status' (for example, two grade 5 research-led departments) to co-operate to jointly review each other's assessment practices.

- Set up a rolling department programme to annually review particular issues of assessment. Rotate this responsibility around individuals or groups in the department. For example you could use the model in part reproduced below, to review your department fieldwork programme. Thus you could use the model to consider whether the tasks set and forms of assessment show clear progression in complexity.

- Clearly there are external levers forcing us down this route. However you can use these levers to take control of the assessment curriculum and change it in the ways you see appropriate. But to do this you will need to create the time to implement the changes.

Excerpts of a model for teaching and assessing group fieldwork projects in higher education (Jenkins, 1997)

Year 1	Year 3
Task tightly defined by staff.	Task largely defined by student group.
Assessment largely formative, helping groups (and individuals in the group) to improve their future performance.	Assessment both formative and clearly summative. Through the (fieldwork) programme students will have been assessed in contexts where all students get the same grade; and where marks are allocated to individuals.
	Through the fieldwork programme students will have evidence they can present to employers of the groupwork skills they have developed.

3.7.6   Staff time, workloads and a department assessment strategy

Perhaps the central difficulty in integrating some of these strategies into our courses is that they (seem to) require us to spend more time on assessment. We may well agree the importance of focusing on assessment in curriculum design and in how we deliver the course. Also, given our own concerns, and the political context in which we work, we understand the need to be rigorous about what we can state about graduate abilities. But we have finite time.

These suggestions largely derive from Gibbs (1994a) and significantly this 'framework' was developed as a group of British academics sought to take Alverno's practices and adapt them to the UK context — including its very different student staff ratios and the pressures for research performance. Gibbs (*ibid*, p.33) argues that "assessment is undertaken for five main reasons:

1.   to motivate students and grab their time and attention — students will often only undertake those study actives which contribute directly to marks or which are formal assessment requirements;

2.   to generate appropriate learning activities — students might, for example never read around and put complex arguments together if they didn't have essays to write;

3.   to give students feedback on their progress and to guide their future learning (formative assessment);

4.   to produce grades, marks and degree classifications (summative assessment);

5.   to produce evidence which can be seen by externals for the purpose of quality assurance."

To me one of the dangers of the current preoccupation with standards is that we will feel forced to focus staff time on functions 4 and 5, for example, through requirements that all assessed work is to be double marked. Because staff time is limited we will perforce have to neglect the vital first three functions with negative impacts on student learning outside class and the quality of student work and graduate standards! Following Gibbs (*ibid*) I suggest that it is essential that a department draw up an assessment strategy where the time available for assessment (Section 3.3) is selectively targeted to the above functions. This might mean:

●   Where the assessment is a central part of the degree classification/graduate record (functions 4 and 5 above) then one has to ensure that these assessments are valid and reliable. This may require selective double marking, careful statistical analysis, and common agreements on explicit criteria and exercises where staff blind mark work and compare implicit criteria. These assessments are where one needs clear codes of conduct for staff and students and where the time of the external examiners is focused.

●   Where the assessment is more concerned with functions 1 to 3 it is important that this stays central to the student experience of the curriculum. Here you can use methods such as self assessment, peer assessment, pass/fail, objective tests, and so on. These are methods that still capture student time and direct their learning but which are less expensive of staff time. This is also where a department can better use postgraduate students (who have less expert judgement) as markers.

- Targeting expensive staff time to certain courses (Section 3.3) which take much time to assess — as in the first-year seminar course at Dartmouth College with its emphasis on coursework essays (Section 3.2.1) — but then ensuring other courses are taught and assessed cheaply.

Clearly staff working individually can't make these decisions. Such changes need a collective departmental focus on assessment. It will require hard choices over targeting staff time and other resources. The alternative is some combination of exhausted staff and/or students who give limited attention to their studies for they are not coherently assessed. For an example of one geography department that has developed an assessment strategy that has sought to save staff time and improve the quality of student work (see Chapman, 1997 for a description of the Aberdeen geography department). When you have developed yours please add it to the GDN Web pages!

3.8 Meeting the needs of students, employers and community groups

"The education system (should) be more responsive to the needs of employment and...ensure that the way that subjects are taught...reflect the needs of students in their subsequent careers rather than the preferences of their teachers."

(Hancock, 1986)

The quotation above represents a radical right 'Thatcherite' critique of the geography curriculum. A related critique of higher education is that it is an industry where the producer (such as academics) controls what is produced (the curriculum) and the needs of students (as consumers) and other interested parties, for example, employers or taxpayers, are ignored. One need not share those political perspectives to recognise that shaping the curriculum is in part a political process, where particular interests are recognised and others rejected or ignored. From this perspective, we ask whose interests and needs should be met through the curriculum. I have already considered how staff research interests can shape the curriculum (Section 3.2). Here I consider how the curriculum can be shaped to meet the needs of students and others, including employers and local community groups.

3.8.1 Meeting students' needs

We, the students themselves, and perhaps their future employers, may decide that students' needs are adequately recognised by other approaches to curriculum design considered here. Thus, students choosing to study geography need a curriculum that provides a sound basis in the discipline (Section 3.1) and an opportunity to learn in a research environment (Section 3.2). Modular structures (Section 3.9) can meet students' needs by giving them some choice over what to study and regular feedback and assessment on their learning. Focusing the curriculum in part around student needs requires us to consider other issues. These include:

- Researching what are student needs. This might mean a rigorous research/ evaluation (Section 3.10) of how students have experienced the curriculum, for example, through 'exit' interviews of students on graduation (and/or x months after graduation) and on their perceptions of whether the curriculum has met their needs.

- A much more systematic investigation (Section 3.9) of student backgrounds and geographic knowledge on entry. On the basis of this information consider redesigning the overall curriculum, or identifying the needs of particular students and helping them to design a curriculum to meet their needs. In the UK this is perhaps becoming more important as students enter from a much wider academic background than previously.

- In some departments, because many students may be entering with only limited expertise in writing essays and analysing a text it may mean that much of the first year curriculum may need to induct them into academic enquiry. See for example the description of the first year geography programme at Liverpool Hope University College (Section 4.1). Such 'learning to learn' and '101 courses' are now a feature of many US universities.

- Redesigning the curriculum in ways that respects that many students need to work in paid employment. This is recognised in, for example, North America through the widespread provision of evening classes, and paying students, through work study programmes, to work on campus and in the department.

- Redesigning the curriculum in ways that reach out to the needs of students who have not been conventionally served by higher education. For example, the Department of Geography at Indiana University developed two innovative programmes, one taught at weekends and the other in a shopping mall, to meet the needs of students (older, women, married and non-white) "who were not well served in their traditional programme" (Bein & East, 1981). Similarly the University of Arizona at Tucson, including the geography programme, has recently developed a range of courses that enable students to graduate by studying solely in the evenings and at weekends (the boxed case study of the Department of Geography at Birkbeck College demonstrates how that curriculum is shaped to meet the needs of mature students).

- Developing courses and programmes that enable graduating students to get professional certification, and which professional organisations recognise as exempting students from aspects of their required professional certification. Such programmes are already important in other disciplines, such as law, business studies and psychology. Clearly in geography such certification can be most readily developed in particular aspects of the discipline and in key transferable skills, for example, the use of information technology.

- Recognising the importance of the hidden curriculum. For example, Hansen *et al.* (1995) offer suggestions on how the curriculum can recognise that women geography graduate students may experience isolation and are uncomfortable in a male-orientated department. They suggest how through , for example, mentoring and building networks, the formal and informal curriculum can better meet their needs.

The above examples are indications of how the curriculum can be investigated and shaped to meet student needs. The particular examples are hopefully useful but it is the approach that is most important.

Curriculum design for part-time mature students

The Geography Department, Birkbeck College, University of London

(for further details see http://www.bbk.ac.uk/Departments/Geography/).

Birkbeck College is an unusual place — certainly for the UK. Its charter and government funding demands that almost all students take their degrees while at the same time holding down a day-time job. This has profound consequences on the nature of the students, the character of the teaching offered, and the basic curriculum offered.

Some factors in the curriculum design for mature students at Birkbeck:

- Students have a mean age of around 29. Their motivations for taking a degree at this age are many. Entry is 'comprehensive' and, more-or-less open to all. This inevitably means that variation in background and ability is high.

- The mode of delivery is not by day release but by instruction in the evening, usually from 18.00 to 21.00 after a normal day's work. In order to deliver anything approaching the number of hours of instruction needed for a degree, students have to study for three nights each week for at least four years. They will also have to be committed to academic work over the greater part of the weekend and the vacations.

- There is at most fifteen hours available each week for classroom contact in each year of the degree programme.

- It is a long time since many of the students left school and the chances are that they did not get on particularly well with academic work when they were there. This has obvious consequences in relation to a general lack of basic study skills. Many mature students have an 'immature attitude' to learning in which it is seen as a quantitative increase in knowledge content, not the acquisition of other qualities. There is security in knowing the 'facts', and many think that it is the duty of staff to lecture such material to them. This makes the introduction of student-centred work difficult. Attitudes to what is, and what is not 'geography' often show a similar immaturity.

- Students lack the opportunity to meet in groups 'out of hours'. Hence some forms of group work can be extremely difficult.

- It is essential to design the curriculum to allow extremely flexible administration, to enable students to take breaks of study in order to deal with the many personal, work and family problems they may encounter.

(cont.)

How is all this reflected in the curriculum?

(Note a distance learning course is now being designed. This description is of the current face-to-face course.)

- Although the programme is for four years, there is a very obvious split between elementary work in Years 1 and 2 and research-led specialisms in years 3 and 4.

- All the first and second year elements are compulsory and are designed to bring students up to a common standard and common knowledge base. Year 1 uses 'Britain's Geographical Development' and 'Global Issues in Geography' as means of introducing the geographical approach to academic study. Field and practical work are integrated into these units. The second year has courses in physical, human and geographical analysis similar to those often taught in other institutions at first year level. There is also a field course unit at this level.

- In the third and fourth year students select from a menu of courses to make up the required number of course units.

- An examination of the course titles on offer show them to be relatively traditional. There is no explicit attempt to teach any underlying philosophy of the subject or modern critical theory. This may well be a response in curriculum content to the demands of the market place as much as it is to timetable and staffing constraints.

- To meet student needs the basic timetable unit is the three-hour evening slot. Most sessions involve a mixture of lecture, discussion and laboratory or other practical work..

- Support materials, in the form of distributed notes, additional reference materials and so on form an important part of the curriculum. These are progressively being made available electronically over the WWW so that students can access them out of hours and if need be out of sequence. Because of work commitments students often miss lectures (careful class registers are kept) and have a need to catch up as quickly as possible.

3.8.2   Meeting the needs of employers and community groups

For many students (and their parents and partners) gaining well paid employment at the end of their geography programme is clearly one of their needs and expectations. How the geography curriculum can achieve that, through developing transferable skills such as working in groups, and through links with employers is considered in detail in the GDN Guide by Chalkley & Harwood (1998). Here I indicate ways in which the geography curriculum can meet these needs:

- A coherent programme of key transferable skills, either delivered integrated into the geography curriculum, or which students can readily study through stand alone modules.

- Formal and informal links with potential employers and employers' organisations.

- A guidance/tutorial system that encourages students to consider and plan their career after college.

- An assessment system that builds up a validated record of student knowledge and skills.

- Modules/courses which consider the changing nature and geography of work and employment and gets students to reflect on the implications for their lives beyond college.

- Providing opportunities for students to work, for paid employment or for credit, in the geography department.

- A statement, written in a language that is clear to employers (including postgraduate courses), of what students can know and do as a result of studying geography in this department.

There are perhaps other groups whose needs should be recognised in the geography curriculum. For those students and for those departments who want a curriculum reflecting social needs, there are examples of innovative geography curricula designed to meet the needs of local community groups. In the 1960s, Bill Bunge's Detroit project tried to empower disadvantaged groups by providing them with access to and opportunity to share in and research their geography, and use that to advocate changes regarding the geography of education (Bunge, 1971). Geography students were involved in this and similar programmes.

In the 1990s there has been a similar push, particularly in the USA to a stronger service orientation to university curricula (Mohan, 1995). For example, Johnson & Oliver (1991) describe a programme in geography and sociology at UCLA which both persuades faculty to orientate their research to socially relevant research on poverty and which trains students with the knowledge and skills to work as professionals in the social services agencies to relieve that poverty. Similarly in the UK Buckingham-Hatfield (1995, p.143) has analysed a range of geography undergraduate programmes, where students work, often for credit, with local community groups "enabling poorly resourced, not for profit, groups to achieve some of their aims".

Politically this is from a very different perspective to the Thatcherite salvo to British geographers which opened this section. However, they both challenge us to ask of our geography curriculum; whose needs does it serve and how can it be designed to meet the needs of those 'we' think are appropriate?

3.9 Modular and credit structures

"As for what passes as a college curriculum, almost anything goes... The major in most colleges is a gathering of courses taken in one department, lacking structure and depth... The curriculum has given way to a market place philosophy... It is as if no-one cared as long as the store stayed open."

(Association of American Colleges, 1985, pp.1-3)

The above quotation illuminates many of the concerns of UK academics about modular, credit-based structures, which are now effectively the norm in the UK, such as the fact they can lack coherence, structure and depth. It also reminds those UK geographers reading this that our colleagues in North America, Australasia and elsewhere have, for a long time, worked in such a structure. Thus much of their philosophy derives from curricular reforms by President Eliot at Harvard University in 1869 (yes, 1869!), which offered students greater choice over what they studied.

At Oxford Brookes University, I have worked in a geography programme that has been modular since 1974. In my view, much of the fears of UK academics about modularity stem from it being pushed through quickly without adequate planning and support. However, we are now in a position to use that experience to maximise the advantages of modular courses and minimise the disadvantages (HEQC, 1996). Here, I assume that we all work in a modular structure and that our task is to make the geography curriculum as effective as possible within that particular institutional structure.

3.9.1   Key features and institutional variations

Modular courses have certain common key features:

- The curriculum is divided up into units or modules.

- Students are assessed and credited at the end of each module. However, there may also be separate synoptic assessments, which at the end of a stage assess the integration of the knowledge learned in these separate units.

- Students are informed of their grades before the next set of modules start, enabling them if necessary, or if they wish, to make changes to that term/semester's programme.

- Students have some choice over their programme of study. Choice may involve combining different disciplines, and also in choosing particular groups of modules (or pathways) offered by a subject team.

- In any programme or module there are likely to be students enrolled from a range of disciplines or programmes.

- Students progressively build up academic credits, and after a certain number and distribution have been accumulated, they obtain a formal qualification.

- Such credits may be transferred between programmes or disciplines within the same institution, and to an extent transferred nationally and perhaps internationally.

However, there are significant institutional variations in modular courses, particularly over the following: the length of a term or semester; whether the course (and an individual module) is defined at two, three or more academic levels; and the numbers of modules necessary to graduate. As a geography department or individual we have limited, or no, say over these structures. So here we start from the recognition that we all work in somewhat distinctive structures and concentrate on those generic strategies that departments and individuals can pursue.

As an academic discipline geography does not have the features that cause some disciplinary groups to react against modularity. For example, we don't have clear boundaries around the discipline; rather we recognise the value of linking our disciplinary knowledge with potentially all disciplines. Just as our individual research interests take us off into all sorts of directions, so we can perhaps better appreciate why our students may choose and gain from doing that. As a discipline we have long agonised over what is 'core', what is central to our conception of geography; and that we have to ensure that our students appreciate what we see, and argue about, as distinctively our conception of geography. Unlike a subject such as civil engineering we are not bound by outside professional requirements to ensure the geography programme contains a particular range of subjects.

Recognising the above, to obtain the advantages of modular structures, the strategies to choose from include:

- Agree on a departmental conception of what is 'core', what is our particular view of geography and ensure through compulsory or synoptic modules (see below) that all students gain an appreciation of that vision. Clearly this links back to our disciplinary concerns (Section 3.1).

- Alternatively, or additionally, encourage students through your course structure (see below) to construct their own course to maximise the choice within and outside geography.

- Recognise the particular opportunities and constraints offered through your institutional and department regulations for geography majors such as (the particular wording will be specific to your institution/department):

Compulsory:	Students have to take and pass this module.
Required:	Students have to take this module. This could mean at one extreme they simply have to: register for the module; it could mean they had to undertake an activity, for example x days fieldwork; or get a certain assessment level, for example, 30%.
Prerequisite:	Students must have taken or passed a specified module or range of modules before they can enrol in a particular module.
Recommended:	Students are counselled to have taken or passed specified modules or be able to…before taking this module.

- Recognise that within your particular institutional structure, there are a range of modular structures you can develop. The best advice is to study how colleagues in other disciplines in your institution have devised their programmes, and see what you can adapt or adopt. Figure 8 (overleaf) indicates that a range of structures to arrange modular programmes are possible, depending upon institutional rules; the basic ideas can also be applied to the design of individual modules.

Figure 8:   *Possible modular structures*

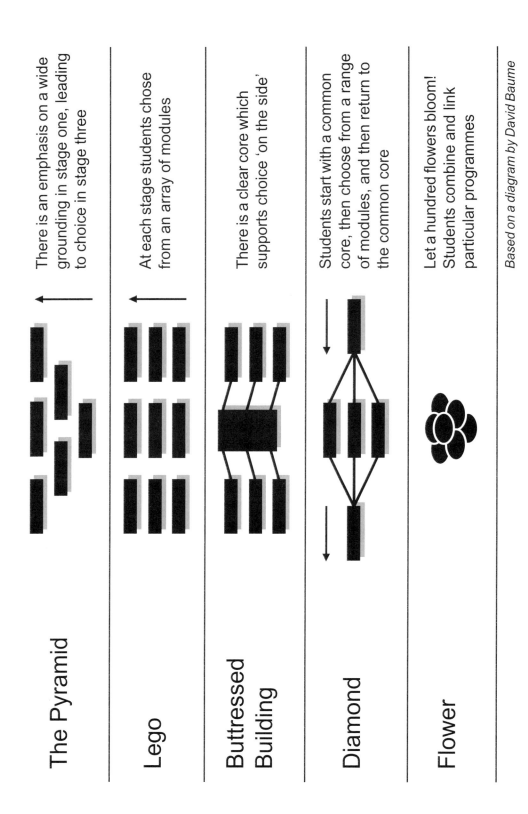

The Pyramid — There is an emphasis on a wide grounding in stage one, leading to choice in stage three

Lego — At each stage students chose from an array of modules

Buttressed Building — There is a clear core which supports choice 'on the side'

Diamond — Students start with a common core, then choose from a range of modules, and then return to the common core

Flower — Let a hundred flowers bloom! Students combine and link particular programmes

Based on a diagram by David Baume

- Recognise that if you want social and/or intellectual coherence it has to be planned in: it won't just happen organically. For example, field courses (even if credited) that just sit outside the rest of the geography programme will be just that — outside. Consider strategies that link field courses into taught classroom courses (see as one example the boxed case study in Section 3.4).

- Make explicit deals between staff as to the amount of teaching required in core modules, where all staff are equally involved or this is the major concern of particular staff, and the amount of teaching that is given over to specialist modules. One of the advantages of modular courses is that staff can pursue teaching closely related to their research interests (Section 3.1).

- Make sure that the department's personal tutor/guidance system/course guides/ WWW pages give students clear and accurate information on which they can make informed choices.

- Consider the use of skills maps, see Figure 9 in the case study of Oxford Brookes University, Section 4.3, to include both disciplinary knowledge and transferable skills and to better ensure integration and coherence of key disciplinary concerns. Skills maps also enable students to make informed choices over what to study.

- Ensure that the assessment system uses a varied range of strategies (see also Sections 3.6 and 3.7) on individual and particular core modules and that the necessity to assess individual modules does not overwhelm staff (Section 3.3).

- Consider the value of synoptic or capstone modules, that is to say modules which require students to integrate their learning across a range of modules and end of degree or course assessment requirements (Jumper, 1992). Here the current experience of colleagues in the USA is particularly relevant, for example, see the theme issue on 'Teaching Sociology' (Wagenaar, 1993) on core and capstone courses. For a geography example see Healey *et al.* (1996).

- Consider maximising the full-time equivalent (FTE) income to the department by ensuring that there is a range of modules which are required/popular for students in other disciplines.

- Consider minimising the costs to the department by making expensive modules, for example, fieldwork modules, only available to students in the geography programme.

What individuals can do:

- If we are mainly used to teaching year-long courses, recognise that in short modules you have to limit the content you attempt to cover. You either have to define the core content that students have to 'master' before they move on, or pick out the key themes which you want students to appreciate, and use a limited area of content to investigate that issue.

- Students need an activity in week one that gets them right into the themes of the module and the way that it will be taught — see boxed example.

An introductory session to a module

A module on *Western Views of China* started with a four-hour session involving the following components:

- an activity in which students read newspaper accounts of the Tiananmen Square 'massacre' of June 1989; the class brainstormed what caused it and from these ideas preliminary causative factors were identified such as 'struggle for political succession' and 'impact of western ideas on students';

- the class was told that the course would be organised around the central question of why the Tiananmen Square events took place, and the way particular western media interpreted what had happened; that there would be an examination question on this issue and that each student would be in a project group to research one of the possible explanations;

- a '*Panorama*' television programme from July 1989 about Tiananmen Square was shown;

- research topics were identified and project teams were established.

By the end of the first session both the central content and the process of the module had been clearly established. The connections to the geography programme were made later in the module.

- Ensure there is a module paper guide (and WWW site) which gives all key details on the course, including assessment arrangements. This better ensures that students know what is expected of them and helps you deal with late comers to the module without taking up your time. Such guides can also set out your subject group's conventions regarding topics such as essay writing. This helps students who are not geography majors know what is expected of them.

- Where students come from a variety of backgrounds consider ways of using that diversity. For example, by ensuring that all student project groups contain at least one member with particular knowledge and/or skill.

- Consider whether we can teach the module in a way that enables students with different backgrounds and interests to find their way through the module, for example, by study packs, guided reading, WWW-based materials and assignments aimed at particular groups of students.

- Adopt strategies to deal with late comers and uncertain numbers of students enrolling in the module, for example: perhaps its better not to put students into project groups in week one; provide audio-tapes or video recordings of previous lectures in a resource centre.

- Recognise that the module taught over 9-15 teaching weeks will develop a momentum and a curriculum of its own. We can help students to see and control that pattern by classroom activities, particularly half-way through a module and towards the end, that push them to integrate what they have learned in the module.

- If we want to help students to make links with other modules, including those in other disciplines, we can do that by constructing particular course work assignments and by short classroom activities, for example, 'Sit with one person who is taking a different set of modules than you this term. Take five minutes each to briefly describe the themes of one of those modules and how it relates to the themes of this module'.

3.10   Classroom research and course evaluation

"The major tenet of classroom research is that college teachers are capable of doing their own research on the questions that interest them."

(Cross & Steadman, 1996, p.13)

"Evaluation is best conceptualised not as something that is done to teachers by experts wielding questionnaires, but as something that is done by teachers for the benefit of their professional competence and their student understanding."

(Ramsden, 1992, p.217)

The curriculum is not fixed: it changes in reaction to a variety of factors from changing staff research interests to changed external requirements and resources. One way staff can control the curriculum is through researching those aspects of the curriculum that interest or concern them and use that information to change the curriculum.

I emphasise this approach to course evaluation because I think it will both empower staff in a context where they feel increasingly controlled. I also think such a research-orientated approach is also more likely to result in staff changing the curriculum in ways that will benefit students. By contrast there is research evidence that the end-of-module student evaluations, that are now compulsory in some institutions, have by themselves little impact on the curriculum (Centra, 1993). However, such evaluations have an importance in signalling to students that they are consulted and are providing evidence to external and internal quality organisations (see Section 1.4) that such procedures are in place. The research evidence is that if end-of-module evaluations are followed by consultation and discussion with peers and educational specialists and action planning they can have a positive impact (Murray, 1997).

What departments can do:

Departments, and individuals, can better ensure that these module evaluations both meet external requirements and have a positive impact on the curriculum if they:

- have a clearly documented and understood policy on end of module evaluations;

- only require such evaluations of fixed modules on a periodic basis (say every 3 years), but requiring such evaluations to be publicly summarised with clear action points which are communicated to students;

- ensure that staff can get appropriate specialist educational advise on how to design and act upon these evaluations;

- have procedures to ensure that such action is taken on the basis of these evaluations and that these are clearly communicated to students;

- outside these firm requirements give individual staff some freedom and support in evaluating aspects of their module that interests them, for example, by evaluating modules half way through when staff and their students can do something about the results;

- have policies for promotion that require staff to have evidence of the results of such evaluations that encourage or require them to take a research or evidenced focus to their teaching (Diamond & Adam, 1993) (Section 3.2).

The above procedures are important. They are likely to have more impact if they operate in a department where the culture and procedures encourage a research and scholarly approach to the curriculum. In the USA such an approach is often termed 'classroom assessment' (Angelo & Cross, 1993) or 'classroom research' (Cross & Steadman, 1996). Elsewhere it might be described as 'action research' (McKernan, 1996), for the focus is less on rigorously designed research for publication and more on information to shape action. This scholarly approach can move from simple but useful techniques, such as those developed by the classroom assessment approach (the book by Angelo & Cross, 1993, has a wide range of techniques from a range of disciplines) to much more rigorous studies that can also be written up as research studies. In the box below are snapshots of geography curricula that demonstrate this approach.

Snapshots of geographic curriculum research

Strachan (1984) from the Department of Geography at the University of Leicester reported on a systematic five year investigation of the geographical knowledge base of first year students surveyed by questionnaire in their first year of university, and what are seen as the implications for curriculum design in the first year. As students increasingly come from such varied backgrounds such an approach might well be adopted by other departments.

Jenkins (1992) from the geography department at Oxford Brookes University investigated the impact on student learning and their approach to studying (Section 3.5) of a workshop-style lecture method and a seen examination. His methodology included selected one-to-one interviews some two years later, and the interviews were at some point prompted by video taped recording of these students in the first lecture of that course.

Long before other UK geography departments had forged links between curriculum and the world of work, Coventry University pioneered a 'sandwich' four year degree, with the third year being in industry. Clark *et al.* (1990) researched whether this had positive impacts on their employment (it did!), the type of careers the students took up and what were the implications for the Coventry curriculum. In a similar vein, Unwin (1986) from Royal Holloway & Bedford New College surveyed employers of the department's graduates of their perceived qualities and the implications for geography curricula.

At the University of Hertfordshire, geography/environmental studies staff have developed an action research strategy, and secured some of the University research income to pursue research on the effectiveness of particular changes to the curriculum, e.g. changes in assessment practice to develop student transferable skills (Blumhof *et al.*,1995).

Proctor & Richardson (1997) of the Santa Barbara department analysed the experimental impact of two multimedia computer modules on student learning. Their study is both of the results and of the experimental research methods used to gauge the impact of these programmes on student learning.

At a different scale Chapman has completed a number of studies of assessment patterns and degree results in British geography, including an analysis of degree results by gender (Chapman, 1994; 1996).

Departments, and to an extent individuals, can encourage this approach to curriculum design by:

- limiting the amount of resources (largely staff and student time) that is spent on end of module evaluations;

- periodically having a forum at which staff and students decide upon the questions that concern them about the current curriculum;

- providing resources, including staff time and money to carry out such investigations; geography departments are well placed to carry out such studies for they are likely to have staff versed in a variety of research methodologies;

- ensuring that the results of these investigations are reported to the department and acted upon, and that such action can include external publication;

So, in conclusion, what are the research questions you want to ask about the curriculum of your department or one of your modules? How might you research and act upon these issues?

Case studies

4.1 Liverpool Hope University College: a value-added curriculum

Department of Environmental and Biological Studies, Liverpool Hope University College, Liverpool, L16 9JD

Contact person: Bill Chambers

Tel.: +44 (0)151 291 3387

Fax.: +44 (0)151 291 3172

E-mail: chambeb@livhope.ac.uk

WWW: http//www.livhope.ac.uk/livhope/gnu

4.1.1   Summary and key features

The geography/environmental studies programme at Liverpool Hope University College was recognised as excellent by TQA assessors for achieving "a high level of added value...as...indicated by a comparison of final awards with qualifications on intake." (HEFCE, 1995). In contrast geography was not entered in the 1996 RAE. Key features of the programme include:

- many of the students on entry have 'low' academic standards and many are mature students with limited formal qualifications;

- the "added value" is achieved by a curriculum that is coherently designed to achieve this;

- resources are targeted to specific areas of the curriculum, in particular, to a seminar programme in the first year; this first year seminar programme, and its potential transferability to other geography departments has been recognised by a Fund for the Development of Teaching & Learning (FDTL) award.

A particular institution

In considering what is 'transferable' from this department, we have to recognise that it is part of a particular institution. Founded from a merger of long-established Catholic and Anglican teacher training institutions, with a high intake of women, Liverpool Hope University College is now developing a distinct institutional mission. This identity includes an emphasis on its Christian foundation, a commitment to opening up access to higher education, including the local community, and developing students with a set of core graduate qualities. Much of its background and contemporary changes echo the development of Alverno College, USA (http://www.alverno.edu/) and links are now being developed between the two institutions. To express this differently, in the context of the developing mass high education system in the UK, Liverpool Hope University College is forging a particular 'market niche', very different from the high prestige, research-orientated University College London (Section 4.2).

The geography programme

Geography is offered as part of a BA/BSc and BEd Combined Studies modular programme. Students take three subjects in their first year, and two subjects in their second and third years. The geography programme contains a core and a range of options reflecting staff interests. It is essentially an undergraduate department with a developing range of masters courses. The description below focuses on particular aspects of the curriculum.

A particular student intake

Many of the students are 'first generation' university students for whom this programme is an induction to university life. The film '*Educating Rita*' (but not the staff/student ratio of 1 to 1!) dramatises and illustrates this experience, including the fact that for many students this experience involves both pain and growth.

About two-thirds of the intake to the geography programme are students entering with low 'A' level scores (12 points average). The open-access philosophy is also demonstrated by admitting students with BTEC/GNVQ qualifications and some with limited paper qualifications, but who at interview demonstrate commitment and potential.

About one-third of the intake are mature students, most of them from local access courses (for example, a non-A-level entry route). There are formal links established with a variety of access programmes in the Merseyside area. Geography staff are involved in teaching and working on a range of these local initiatives, many of which receive EU funding.

There are also projects with inner-city schools to target entry to those students who could benefit, but are not likely to obtain the normal 12 point entry.

Some 60-70% of the geography students are women.

Reach Out

Reach Out is a new College initiative — a geography degree programme for local mature students is taught in the community, in partnership with local schools and community centres. As yet only on a small scale, it symbolises the department's access philosophy.

4.1.2 Aspects of the year one programme

Targeting Resources

Section 3.3 of this Guide considers the generic issue of a department choosing where to target scarce resources, particularly staff time. Operating at an overall staff:student ratio (SSR) of 1:21, the geography first year programme is resourced at one hour of staff contact to two hours of student learning. This is an example of 'front loading' the curriculum, with the aim of developing in students the capabilities/knowledge that will enable them to work with less staff support in years two and three. The first year is also front loaded qualitatively: most of the teaching in the first year is done by the more experienced, teacher-trained staff.

Resources (such as staff time, including that of support staff, and the department budget for printing) is also targeted to a compulsory core, which runs through the three years of the degree. The description below focuses on aspects of this core and ignores, because of space the other elements of the programme.

Aspects of the year one core

Attendance

Attendance at all taught sessions is required and monitored. Students who, without prior notification, miss more than two sessions are interviewed by staff. This is presented not as punishment but as an indication that something is going wrong with the student's experience of the curriculum and that staff support may be required. Given the particular student intake, where often there are major initial cases of lack of self-confidence, many combining college with parenting, employment and so on., such intervention is seen as central to developing student autonomy and ensuring a high completion rate.

A year one seminar programme

Running through year one all geography students take an intensive well-resourced seminar programme. The programme aims to develop, through geography, key learning skills that will enable students to succeed in the rest of their course and which will subsequently aid employability, such as: how to research and write essays; to analyse a text; and the related transferable skills of working in groups and making spoken presentations. Features of this programme include:

- Students are taught in small groups of 10-12 (by contrast other first year courses may well be in large lectures).

- Those teaching on the programme are amongst the most able/experienced staff.

- The seminar programme is supported by quality relatively well-funded materials.

- Much of the emphasis is on confidence-building with all key activities, for example, giving an individual spoken presentation, preceded by careful training and followed up by one to one feedback.

- The TQA assessors strongly commended this programme for meeting student needs. A successful bid to the FDTL programme aimed at developing the programme and its materials for adaption by other geography departments (see WWW site listed above).

- In the first year students get a linked training programme which develops key IT based skills, such as word processing, using spreadsheets and geography databases.

Fieldwork

All first year geography students go on the equivalent of a week's field course. Again this involves targeting staff resources. Recognising the particular and varied needs/ circumstances of students, they are given three alternatives: they can go on a series of day trips costing them c.£30; a residential field course in North Wales, c.£60; a foreign location such as Romania or the French Alps, c.£120.

4.1.3   Aspects of the stage two programme

Compulsory Core

The first year seminar core and the field course programme is progressively built on in the second and third years by two compulsory courses.

All second year students take a research methods module, which includes 5 days of fieldwork. As with the seminar programme in year one this is taught in small seminar groups (12-16 students) by experienced staff, with well resourced learning packages. Its aim is to develop students' ability to understand and to carry out geographic research. Thus it includes input and assessed activities on questionnaire design and analysing data. It builds on the first year fieldwork programme where students work in groups under staff designed and directed one-day research projects. In this second year programme, students work and are assessed as a group, with the project largely designed by them with staff acting as advisers and part as directors. As well as this assessed group report, students also have to present an individual assessed plan for their third year dissertation. In the third year these research skills are further developed and tested by all students doing an individual dissertation.

Internationalisation of the curriculum

Most students come with a background with limited or no experience of foreign travel (though Liverpool is a city of many migrant streams and cultures). The curriculum is designed to give all students some international experience. In the first year some 60-70% of students opt for the foreign field course. Through a student exchange programme those students doing the Welsh field course will be joined by a group of Romanian students. Strong links have been established with the geography department at Bucharest University and there are student and staff exchanges with Romanian staff teaching on the geography programme. Also links and student exchanges have been established with Eastern and Western Europe and the USA. This internationalisation operates both through the formal curriculum and what was described in Section 1.2 as the co-curriculum, that is to say the informal curriculum outside the structure of formal courses.

Development of careers/employability

A focus on developing student employability is developed through the core skills/research methods core that has already been described. A focus on employability is also developed through:

- a compulsory end of second year, 3-week work placement, organised by the department using discipline-based contacts;

- in 1996-97 a pilot work-based learning module was initiated by the department as part of an institution-wide initiative.

What is the evidence of added value?

Student satisfaction. As well as an evaluation of all modules to a consistent format there are periodic evaluations across a student cohort. These all demonstrate high levels of student appreciation of the curriculum.

Degree classifications/student employability

These demonstrate high added value. The 1996 graduates had entered with a mean 10.5 points at A level with 25% non-traditional entry. There was a 95% completion rate with 3% getting a first and 26% an upper second. None failed. The first destination statistics showed that within six months of graduation 48% were employed and 22% doing further study.

4.1.4   What of this is transferable to other geography departments?

Perhaps nothing. Perhaps this is so particular an institution or this is not the 'market niche' you think appropriate to your department. However, here are some suggestions:

- Any department should be very clear what outcomes it wants to achieve, and then ensure that the curriculum is coherently targeted to that end. In that sense the UCL geography curriculum (Section 4.2) is, in a radically different form, an example of the same principle.

- Target resources (Section 3.3) to meet the particular student needs (Section 3.8) you identify.

- In the context of cuts in already limited resources ensure that somewhere in each year of the programme there is 'quality time' for students and staff, which will keep students in the programme, give staff job satisfaction and develop high-level learning.

- Develop effective mechanisms for ensuring that all students are well known by at least one member of staff.

- Ensure that there are effective structures in the curriculum for developing student autonomy.

4.2 University College London: a research-led department

Department of Geography, University College London, 26 Bedford Way, London WC1H 0AP

Contact person, Ray Harris

Tel.: 0171-380-7583

Fax.: 0171-380-7565

WWW: http://www.geog.ucl.ac.uk

4.2.1   Summary and key features

The Department of Geography at UCL in its self-assessment claim for excellence in the TQA argued that "teaching and learning take place in a top rated research department" (Department of Geography, 1994, p.1). The claim for excellence was supported by the assessors who were impressed "by the way the scholarship and research interests of the academic staff directly support teaching and enhance the student learning experience." (HEFCE, 1995b, para. 23). In the 1996 RAE the department got a 5-star rating — the highest possible grade. Key features of the current (1997) undergraduate curriculum include:

- an emphasis on developing students knowledge of, and ability to contribute to, geographic research;

- staff research interests directly shaping the undergraduate curriculum, particularly in years 2 and 3;

- staff time devoted to undergraduate teaching being planned to ensure that staff have adequate time to undertake high level research and to teach (new) postgraduate courses.

While the focus of this description is on how this research focus in part directs the curriculum, it needs to be seen as but one of three identified areas of student needs (Section 3.8) that should shape the curriculum. In the curriculum review (see below) the needs identified were: liberal education, vocational development and geographical research understanding. Their common thread is to develop independent study skills and critical thinking through geographical study.

4.2.2   Levers for change

Until recently the basic features of the curriculum had remained constant since the early 1980s. Certain factors prompted a major review in 1996. Key levers for change were:

- criticisms by the TQA assessors that the curriculum should "demonstrate progressions from year to year more conspicuously and address the concerns the assessors share with some of the external examiners that the lack of a compulsory core in the second year can lead to a loss of a distinctive subject identity"; relatedly the assessors urged that the third year dissertation which was then optional be made "a compulsory third year course" (HEFCE, 1995b, paras. 23-24);

- awareness that to succeed in the next RAE and in bids for external research, a more strategic and collective approach to research would need to be further developed;

- a recognition that, with undergraduate numbers capped, growth in income through teaching would have to be obtained by increasing post-graduate student numbers and developing new taught masters programmes;

- a recognition that the tradition of widespread student choice and interactive teaching would have to be limited to release staff time;

- coincidentally, geography was required by university procedures to review its departmental strategy for research and teaching.

The over-riding aim of the review of the undergraduate curriculum was, while building in key features of quality, to protect staff time which could be devoted to research and other scholary activities; quality was largely conceived as developing students knowledge of/ ability to do research and study independently. Central to the review was a considered costing of the then curriculum and the revised curriculum (Section 3.3).

Key features of the pre- and post-1996 curriculum are set out in Table 3 below.

Table 3: *Curriculum change at UCL*

Main Features of pre 1996 Curriculum	**Main Features of Post 1996 Curriculum**
Year one: included several courses integrating physical and human geography as well as compulsory practical data processing skills.	***Year one:*** compulsory unit in data collection and interpretation. Students choose from a series of optional units.
Year two: Series of whole year units each taught by 2 staff from which students had an open choice.	***Year two:*** Students required to take common methodology unit, and one of either a human or physical geography unit which further develops research techniques for the compulsory dissertation in year 3. Also students choose from a series of half units which cover systematic subjects and relate to the research interests of staff.
Year three: Student choose from a series of half units generally taught by one member of staff around their research interests. There was an optional dissertation.	***Year three:*** Compulsory dissertation. Students choose from a series of half units, reflecting staff interests, organised by research groups.

Staff time to do research is protected by the following strategies:

- Every three or four years staff are entitled to a one-term sabbatical. If they have had a heavy administration load, for example, as the undergraduate or admissions tutor, the sabbatical may be for two terms.

- The previous year-long second year units have been replaced by a greater number of half units which are largely lecture-based and often assessed by examination only.

- While the overall planning of the curriculum and teaching responsibilities is done by a Curriculum Development Group, the Research Groups will take increasing responsibility for co-ordinating those units for which they are responsible, particularly the specialist units in the third year. Such team teaching enables staff to collectively arrange to cover those staff on sabbaticals and those who need to be away from college in term time, and to arrange an individual's teaching in concentrated blocks.

- The close connection between the content of the curriculum and staff research better ensures that when staff have time to do research they have been thinking on these questions.

- To further protect academic staff time, the department is appointing five Teaching Assistants on the North American model to support much of the teaching of techniques, fieldwork and so on, and perhaps some of the administration of large courses.

- Staff teaching 'load' has also been acknowledged by crediting learning which had previously not been credited. The department has long emphasised a system of small group tutorials in all years; this resource, which is an expensive form of teaching, has been retained but now counts for a half credit in the first year and is associated with dissertation training and completion in the second and third years.

Students awareness of the process of geographic research is developed by:

- In term one of the first year, all tutorial groups interview a member of staff. The explicit aim of this exercise (see box below) is to make students aware of the process of geographic research and the role of research in this department. Effectively students are being acculturated into the ethos of a research-led department through a resource-intensive front loading of the curriculum (Section 3.3) [the exercise was originally developed by Denis Cosgrove at what was then Oxford Polytechnic (1981) as part of a third year synoptic module].

- In the second year and particularly in the third year, many of the systematic modules are closely based upon staff research and the research groups in the department. These include analyses of research methodology and progressively develop the students' ability to do geographic research (see next section).

Introductory exercise/module on understanding the role of research in geography

In the first year all students have a weekly tutorial in groups of 4. This describes one of the tutorial exercises in term one.

- As part of the compulsory 'Ideas in Geography' module each tutorial group is allocated to a member of staff (not their tutor).

- Their task is to interview and write a report on that persons' research.

- The objectives for the project include learning about "the aims, methods and ideas of **geographers doing research in the department**; to find out why and how research projects are started, how they are carried out, and how they are turned into publications…and to discover more about the **relationships between geographical research and teaching**" (emphasis in instructions to students).

- To prepare for the interview students are given, by the member of staff, a current CV and 'three pieces of writing which are representative of their research, one of these pieces will be an unpublished manuscript'.

Students' ability to **do** research is developed primarily by a series of compulsory courses in years one through three.

- In the first year students take a compulsory unit in the principle and practice of geographical data collection, analysis and interpretation. This is a well resourced unit entirely assessed by course work essays and exercises. It also includes a residential 7 day field course.

- Second year students take two well-resourced units which explicitly aim to develop their ability to undertake geographic research. In terms one and two all students take a course on the practice of geography: 'The course will familiarise students with debates over the practical conduct of geographic research, including undergraduate dissertation research'. Entirely assessed by course work, the two main requirements are: a) a comparative central appraisal of how a research topic has been carried out by different researchers; and b) towards the end of term 2 students present, both orally for presentation in tutorials and as a paper, a proposal for a third year dissertation.

- Second year students can take individual modules in research methods in physical geography, human geography, or in both subject areas.

- All third year students registered for single honours are required to do a half unit dissertation. They can choose to extend this to a full unit out of the three and half units required in that year.

4.2.3   What of this is transferable to other geography departments?

Perhaps none. This after all is an internationally recognised, large department. However, here are some suggestions:

- Being very explicit about the key goals of the department (research recognition) and then ensuring that the undergraduate curriculum supports that key goal. In that respect the value added curriculum at Liverpool Hope University College (Section 4.1) is but another example of the same principle.

- If we want to develop understanding of geographic research, then it needs to be coherently and progressively developed through the curriculum. It won't just happen because 'elsewhere' staff are doing research.

- In the context of limited resources, there is a case for carefully targeting a high level of resources to particular areas, while limiting resources to other areas of the curriculum. The case study of Liverpool Hope University College, in a very different context, also demonstrates this principle — aspects of the UCL approach can be adopted in very different resource contexts.

- Recognise the career potential of this approach. We live in an information society and many jobs are based on the collection, analysis and presentation of information. Building this research focus into the curriculum can aid student employability. This might mean including activities which develop students ability to carry out contract research for clients and forging close links with companies who employ graduates with these skills (see Section 3.2).

4.3 Oxford Brookes University: an integrated curriculum

Author: Judy Chance, Oxford Brookes University

Geography Department, School of Social Sciences and Law, Oxford Brookes University, Gipsy Lane, Oxford OX4 2DD

Contact person: Judy Chance (jchance@brookes.ac.uk)

Tel: 01865-483750

Fax: 01865-483937

4.3.1   Key features

Oxford Brookes currently offers two single fields in the Geography Department: geography and physical geography. The latter is a new development, recruiting its first intake in 1997. Most of the following case-study relates to the longer established geography field, since it illustrates more effectively the ways in which we have modified curriculum design in response to the multiple forces acting on our particular ouija board.

The geography curriculum at Oxford Brookes University is integrated in two particular senses: firstly we have historically rejected the physical/human divide in favour of a social/ environmental focus. Secondly, we have a tradition of integrating the development of transferable skills into the academic development of our students.

4.3.2   The modular course at Oxford Brookes University

Geography is a single field subject, that is, all of our students are studying another subject, making up a joint Honours programme. The range of fields combined with geography is high, up to 29, although certain combinations are particularly popular. We therefore cannot assume that all our students have access to the same range of opportunities within the University, to say nothing of their extra-curricular lives.

Currently students must pass at least eight modules in their first year, and a further 16 over the next two years. Most fields, including geography, have three compulsory modules in year one. The minimum sixteen modules taken over the next two years must be acceptable to one or other field, and must include at least seven from each field. Some, but not all, fields include a compulsory core of modules; this is the approach adopted in geography.

4.3.3   Core programme

Why have a core?

In some senses a compulsory core runs counter to the ideal of flexible course design offered by a modular course, so why do we make six of our modules (over half of our graduates' exposure to geography) compulsory? Our reasons include:

- to ensure progression in academic development by looking at a central set of issues with an increasing level of knowledge and abstraction;

- to develop all the transferable skills identified as essential both by the University and by employers;

- to ensure that students entering year one with a wide range of backgrounds (we don't require geography at A-level) acquire a common grounding to prepare them for the next two years;

- to ensure that students develop their research skills before they have to start work on their dissertations;

- to involve all staff in collaborative team teaching on the core;

- to demonstrate the integrative nature of a discipline which is all too often seen as divided into mutually incomprehensible specialisms;

- to reflect the staff belief in the central importance of an understanding of environmental change and environmental policy for our graduates.

The design of the core curriculum started from these broad concerns. Having allocated six modules to the core, three in year one, and three over the next two years, the next issue is to design an overall set of aims and objectives, and to allocate particular skills, topics, approaches and resources to each core module.

The core in year one

The first year programme introduces the particular social/environmental focus of the whole course, moving from high profile global issues such as global warming and deforestation to more detailed study of more local issues such as coastal flooding in Wales. The final term introduces students to planning, carrying out and analysing their own local research projects. Transferable skills are also built into the programme, with each module emphasising two key areas:

Term One: group work and formal writing

Term Two: word processing and oral presentation

Term Three: numeracy and field-based research

The first year programme is largely delivered via small group teaching, with weekly seminar sets (8-12 students) using workbooks. The high level of staffing is seen as an early investment to produce confident students capable of more independent learning in the later stages of the course. In the early days the seminars were all led by permanent staff, but more recently the increased research funding and pressure to produce publications has led to increased reliance on part-time support from postgraduate students, supplemented by a student-link co-ordinator (Section 3.3.4).

The core in years two and three

The second and third year core modules pick up the same themes and skills, and develop them at a more advanced level.

The main fieldwork module (year two, terms two and three) gives student groups much more autonomy in designing projects, with increased reliance on students seeking supervision, rather than scheduled classroom contact. This approximates more closely to their preparation for their dissertation, but working in small groups (four or five) offers more peer support, as well as addressing some basic health and safety issues. While the fieldwork is essentially geographical in focus, the project choices often reflect the influence of students' other fields. This freedom to build bridges between disciplines is seen as a valuable element of any joint Honours programme, especially when one field is as wide-ranging a discipline as geography.

The other two core modules are in the third year. They build on the study of environmental change and environmental management to include an exploration of the politics of pollution production and control (term one) and a more conceptual analysis of the wide range of value systems which underpin social attitudes to the environment in different places and cultures (term three). In the closing stages of the core increasing precedence is given to academic development, on the assumption that transferable skills development has largely been taken care of already, and that further use of techniques, allied to the regular use of assessment by staff, peers and self, encourages greater sophistication and fluency.

4.3.4   Optional modules

Why offer options?

The original attraction of the modular course was the freedom it offered students to construct their own degree programmes. This remains highly valued, although decreasing resources and increasing student numbers have led to a loss of choice: students now do fewer modules than in the past (a minimum of 24 now, compared to 27 for those graduating in 1997, and 30 for those graduating in 1985). Conversely, the workload for each module has risen, with more emphasis on independent learning.

The reasons for offering options include:

- different students have different interests and needs; this relates to academic content, teaching styles and transferable skill development;

- staff have different research interests and areas of expertise;

- geography is such a diverse discipline that no student can hope to cover all aspects, so choice is essential;

- some options are less resource-hungry than others;

- adopting relevant modules taught by other fields allows a small team to offer a wider ranging programme;

- flexibility (even in its currently limited form) remains a selling point when recruiting students;

- some specialist modules offer specific professional skills.

Designing specialist curricula

Specialist modules are taught by individual staff members and are driven primarily by academic concerns. Because all staff team-teach on the core, and because of a common approach to teaching and learning, the delivery and underlying social-environmental concerns reflect the philosophy of the core. This provides coherence, and was recognised as a common strand by students in a recent evaluation of their whole student experience.

Mapping skills

The use of a skills map (Figure 9) has helped us to identify where particular skills are taught, practised and assessed in both core and options. It has also pointed to some gaps in provision, which can be addressed in curriculum modifications. The skill categories are set by the University, as part of an Enterprise Programme. Each student is encouraged to build up a personal profile of their skills development, using the skills map to identify what they have already achieved, and to help to select modules which will contribute to more complete profile.

Placing of modules

In order to maximise flexibility, no specialist modules are restricted to only one year of the programme, although some are recommended for second or third year, depending on their academic challenge, and their reliance on key skills or knowledge acquired at certain phases of the core. The structure gives each staff member one light term a year, that is, a term in which they are not leading the delivery of any modules. This is seen as essential if staff are to continue as active researchers, and are to integrate their research into their teaching.

Figure 9: *Skills matrix*

This matrix indicates the transferable skills which are taught (T), practised (P) and assessed (A) in the core programme at Oxford Brookes University (2604, 2605, 2642 and 2662 are the compulsory core modules). Students use the matrix to help them to construct a profile of their skills acquisition. A parallel matrix of skills in optional modules also exists, and students use this to help them in their choice of modules. It allows them to consider their development of key skills alongside issues relating to academic coherence of their programme.

The module is also helpful for staff, since it allows easy identification of any skills areas which are insufficiently taught, practised or assessed.

In addition it is of use to employers, in that it can be used alongside a graduate's course transcript to provide validated evidence of skills development.

Skill Category	Component	2604	2605	2608	2642	2662
Self management	Clarify values	P A	T	T P		T P
	Set goals	T P			T P A	
	Manage time	T P A	A	P	T P A	
	Assess self	T P		A	P	
Learning skills	Independence	P A	T A		P A	P A
	Co-operation	T P A	T A	P		
	Range of strategies		T P A			
Information skills	Literature search	T P A	A	T	P A	P A
	Information retrieval	T P A	A	T P	P A	P A
	Information handling	T P A	A	T P A	P A	P
	Referencing	T P A	A	P	P	P
Teamwork	Taking responsibility	P A	T P A	P	P A	P
	Taking initiative	P A	A	P	P A	P A
	Negotiation	P A	T P	P	P A	P A
	Team evaluation	T P A	T P		T P A	
Problem solving	Analysis	T P A	T P A		P A	P
	Lateral thinking		T P A			
	Setting questions	T P A	T P A		T P A	T P A
	Identifying strategies	T P A	T P A		T P	P A
	Evaluating success	T P A	T P A		T P	T P A
Communication	Reading/listening		T P A	T P A	P	T P A
	Choice of styles	P A	T P A	T P A	P A	T P A
	Coherent argument		T P A	P A	P A	P A
	Analysis	T P A	T P A	P A	P A	P
	Synthesis		T P A			T P A
	Self evaluation	T P A	T P A			
	Peer evaluation	T P A	T P			
	Author evaluation		T P A		P A	

4.4 Virtual Geography Department

Author: Judy Chance, Oxford Brookes University

Department of Geography, University of Texas at Austin, Austin, Texas

Contact person: Ken Foote

WWW: http://www.utexas.edu/depts/grg/virtdept/contents.html

4.4.1   Summary and key features

The department has been set up to link existing geography departments in the United States. Its function is primarily linked to teaching, rather than research. The production of high quality teaching materials using cybermedia is the major focus. The collaborative nature of the department allows a sharing of the time and resources dedicated to developing new materials, but also has major design implications: materials must be sufficiently flexible to fit into the teaching approaches and curricula of a wide range of institutions.

A wider concern is the pressure for universities to acknowledge the need for radical changes in their structure (organisational and physical) to benefit from the opportunities presented by cyberspace. In particular, the current model of co-location of faculty members is no longer necessary, when contact in cyberspace is so easy. Students also are freed from old constraints, and can access materials from many more sources. Their learning needs to be supported in new ways, to make sure that the materials are as well designed and as easy to find as possible.

4.4.2   Goals

The department has three main goals, and three subsidiary ones:

- Develop staff skills in creation and use of hypermedia resources.

- Develop new models of teaching and curriculum design using hypermedia which can support the future development of other virtual departments and universities.

- Facilitate the transition from the WWWs current ad hoc nature to a more ordered structure, in which resources are easier to find.

- Establish appropriate methods of review and evaluation for hypermedia resources.

- Create a uniform method for citing and crediting the authors of such resources.

- Create a uniform method for indicating and confirming the sources of such resources.

4.4.3   Development of the Virtual Department

The first stages have involved a series of summer workshops (1996-1998), attended by 30 faculty members drawn from 30 different institutions. Staff attending the two-week workshops have four aims:

- To become familiar with the structure of the Virtual Department.

- To prepare a development plan for the module they are producing.

- To learn HyperText Mark-up Language (HTML) for the production of on-line materials.

- To get the first unit of their module on-line.

4.4.4   Structure of the curriculum

The Virtual Department has an ambitious brief for its curriculum, with goals set for both the whole department and for individual modules:

- Provide complete coverage of all topics and regions.

- Embody the synthetic and integrative nature of the discipline.

- Make on-line, interactive review and evaluation a central feature.

- Support a range of teaching and learning strategies.

- Make use of cybermedia fundamental to each module.

- Adopt a flexible modular format for a range of users.

- Index all material by keywords for easy searching.

4.4.5   Current curriculum

The Virtual Department has no over-arching curriculum, because its materials are designed to slot into the degree programmes taught at any department which chooses to make use of the materials. Each module is designed by a working group, using a common format and agreed protocols of lay-out, referencing and hyper-text links. The working groups cover the following topics:

- cultural geography

- earth's environment and society

- GIS/cartography/remote sensing/statistics

- history and philosophy of geography

- introductory human geography

- physical geography

- regional and area studies

- urban and economic geography

- virtual field trips

- world regional geography

Each working group is responsible for producing a set of modules which are free-standing, and can be adapted with minimum difficulty to fit into the range of teaching programmes adopted by any institution wishing to make use of the resources available. The common format and guidelines on presentation of materials help to encourage use of more than one module, since much of the teachers' learning about the Virtual Department's approach is carried out in their use of the first module which they select. This transferability will also apply to students using the materials.

4.4.5   Resource implications

Once the modules are complete and freely available, they offer one way in which to increase the range of specialist options available to students, especially those in smaller departments which do not have enough staff to cover all aspects of geography. Their main use, however, seems likely to be as a supplement to existing courses, rather than a substitute.

The system may be of especial value in reaching out to students who otherwise do not have access to higher education and/or to other students. This would apply to students on courses such as those run by the Open University, whose contact with both staff and other students is increasingly being eroded by reductions in funding. It would also apply to students who, for any reason, cannot easily travel to University or to fieldwork sites.

While virtual fieldwork, as it currently exists, cannot hope to replace actual fieldwork, training can use virtual fieldwork to prepare students for their real fieldwork, thus minimising time spent on unnecessary learning in the field, that is, learning which can be done somewhere else. As both students and institutions find the cost of fieldwork increasingly burdensome, greater efficiency in the time spent in the field may help to preserve this vital part of the geography curriculum.

Another potential advantage is the exposure to topics and approaches other than those familiar, not only in a single institution, but at a national level, given the different cultures of geography which exist in different countries. If an appropriately validated set of course materials exists, and if systems of credit transfer can be established, the Virtual Department could become a pioneer for a global 'cyberuniversity', offering the advantages of a student body with a wide range of skills and experiences, and therefore with the potential to teach each other and the staff involved to ask new questions and follow new paths.

4.4.6   International extensions?

Clearly there is a potential to extend the virtual geography department worldwide. There is the precedent with the NCGIA Core Curriculum in GIS — which provides key course content written by leading experts world-wide for adapting to local courses (http://bbq.ncgia.ucsb.edu:80/giscc/)

5 Summary and conclusions: changing the curriculum

"...care and quality are internal and external aspects of the same thing. A person who sees quality and feels it as he works is a person who cares. A person who cares about what he sees and does is a person who's bound to have some characteristics of quality."

(Pirsig, R.M., 1976, p.269)

"It is no secret that faculty sometimes find it difficult to work together for curriculum improvement. In fact in many colleges there is little formal discussion of the curriculum except under the greatest duress. And when discussions do occur participants tend to argue from varied positions without spelling them out... Such discussions frequently become contentious. It is no wonder that curriculum development work is not popular work among college faculty."

(Stark & Lattuca, 1997, p.9)

Some colleagues who have read draft versions of this Guide wanted a more prescriptive tone and a conclusion which said this is what a quality geography curriculum is and this is the way to create it. Perhaps I am overstating their argument, but if so let me use it to make explicit the approach taken in this Guide.

The perspective offered here is that there is no absolute conception of quality; in the buzz words of many management gurus 'quality' is 'fitness for purpose', or has to be worked out by geographers individually and collectively to meet the needs of the particular students they teach. Thus, I purposefully chose as case studies departments and institutions with very contrasting conceptions of quality. What unites them is that they have carefully defined that quality and rigorously ensured that the various elements of the curriculum cohere to create that vision.

Similarly I rejected the view of some educationalists and quality organisations that there is one way to build the curriculum, in particular to start by defining one's aims and objectives, rather I likened the building of a curriculum to our taking control of a ouija board and the forces we recognise as shaping the curriculum. I believe that academics are more likely to improve their teaching, and here in particular the geography curriculum, if they are given options to choose from and prioritise in terms of their particular circumstances and interests. Clearly there are value judgements in the forces recognised here, but by purposefully not prioritising them I assume you will decide what weight to give them as individuals or as a department.

What I am prescriptive about is the view that teaching and curriculum design is an act of scholarship, and that as academics when we teach we demonstrate the value of universities to society and immediately our students by the extent to which we are aware of and use the conversations on the scholarship of the curriculum. If we treat curriculum design as something that can be done just by common sense, knowledge and experience, why should we expect others to value the knowledge we have developed on the *substantive* areas we teach? So this Guide has been written to demonstrate some of the scholarship and research on teaching and course design. Such then has been the approach taken, but to conclude here are some practical suggestions on taking some of these ideas forward.

What individuals can do:

- Start small and simple. While being aware of the complexity introduced, and the varied factors that can be considered, I suggest that you first focus on one area that concerns you, for example, 'how can I get my students to work effectively outside class?'. That could result in a radical change to the curriculum or it may be appropriate to introduce one or two key changes to your module. To be prescriptive, probably the main area to consider is the way you assess students to signal the importance of out of class learning.

- Treat the changes as an experiment or an intellectual puzzle. Be open to the possibility that it may not 'succeed' the first time.

- Involve your students. Tell them of the changes you are making and why.

- Involve your students by researching and evaluating the changes. Get them involved in considering and researching their learning. One source I strongly commend you adapt is the range of 'classroom assessment' techniques set out in Angelo & Cross (1993).

- Be open to change your approach and the particular revisions you are making.

- Document what you are doing. To convince others, perhaps in particular your colleagues and perhaps your students, you may need strong evaluation evidence of the impact of the changes you are making.

Suggestions for a department:

To be prescriptive a department needs to act collectively. In some circumstances that collectivity may have to be forced through by 'managerial action'; hopefully it can be developed co-operatively as then the changes are likely to have greater impact, and will also draw on everyone's expertise. What is not acceptable or tenable is the individualism that has long characterised curriculum design. Clearly there were and are strengths in that individualism that need to be retained and fostered. However, the research evidence is compelling as to the multiple factors that determine what students learn and the impact on them of college (Pascarella & Terenzini, 1991). Accordingly we have to ensure that the various elements of the curriculum cohere to create the maximum positive impact. Also, given the pressures on staff, in particular the multiple demands on our limited time, it is critical for our own health and sense of doing a worthwhile job that as a department we act collectively. Again what unites the case studies is that they have done that and, of course, that has involved managing conflict and is never complete.

5.1 A useful analogy

One way for a department to conceive the process of building or changing the curriculum is the analogy developed by Ifan Shepherd of the Middlesex geography department and David Unwin of Birkbeck College (Gold *et al.*, 1991). The analogy is with designing software: some software is designed on a top-down principle, first devising the overall conception before designing separate units. This is considered particularly appropriate to large complex hierarchical products. By analogy, a department using this approach might start by agreeing on its graduate profile — what students should be able to do as a result of studying geography in this department — or it might start by agreeing that over the next three years the department's focus has to be on raising income from postgraduate courses. By analogy with complex software products this approach might be more appropriate to a large department or where there is a strong undergraduate curriculum committee.

A contrasting approach to software design is to celebrate the flair of individual designers and argue that software (a curriculum) designed in a top-down fashion will lack creativity, inventiveness and the commitment of individuals. If 'managing academics is like herding cats', we should celebrate their cat-like features and their fascination with the particular subject matter. That approach to departmental curriculum planning would start by each member of the teaching staff defining the areas of the curriculum they want to teach and then building up incrementally from these separate decisions. Recognising that 'cats do come when food is put out', they could decide what rewards there could be for effective involvement in this process and with collaborating on aspects of the curriculum.

A third approach to software design and curriculum change is a 'middle out' approach which some consider combines the strong features of the two other approaches. In software design one concentrates on the middle tiers of a product, moving iteratively up and down the design process. A department in using this strategy would start by defining the middle tiers; research techniques, the first year programme, specialist options, the current assessment strategy and so on. One then moves iteratively up and down the scales, at times concentrating on the overall shape and at other points getting individuals or groups to specify the modules for which they have particular responsibility. This was the approach used by the Department of Geography at the University of Canterbury, New Zealand during a major curriculum review. Here, to ensure a more collective approach, individuals were moved between different design teams.

I have no prescription as to which of these approaches are appropriate to your department, but conclude with some suggestions for departmental actions, which clearly echo those for individual action.

- Start with limited changes. While being aware of the complexity introduced, the varied factors that can be considered, I suggest that you first focus on one or more particular areas that immediately concern you, for example, ensuring that the curriculum is managed to ensure that staff have time to do research.

- A more ambitious approach would be to agree that members of the department are divided into design teams each to consider one of the forces identified in the ouija board and report back. In the box below is an edited version of one of the suggested design tasks for the workshop that links to this Guide. Clearly it could be developed by a department for use outside a workshop. The value of this approach is that it would give the department a full sense of the issues and options. In a way it is a bottom-up approach to design. However, you will then probably have to prioritise the 'forces' to act upon.

- Develop a timetable or programme for change. One way would be to initially decide on what a graduate should be able to do as a result of studying geography in this department, then to focus on year one, or perhaps to analyse how the current assessment supports or fails to support that sense of 'graduateness' and then...

- Involve your students. Tell them of the changes you are making and why.

- Involve your students by researching and evaluating the changes. Get them involved in considering and researching their learning. The general approach I recommend is that of action or classroom research (Cross & Steadman, 1996; McKernan, 1996), and where aspects of the department's research strategy directly researches the impact of the curriculum.

- Be open to change your approach and the particular changes you are making.

- Document what you are doing. To convince others perhaps, in particular, internal and external quality agencies and perhaps your students; you will need strong evaluation evidence of the impact of the changes you are making.

Good Luck!

A possible action plan

To speculatively (re)design the curriculum in this department

Divide staff in the department into groups each of which is responsible for one or more of the strategies from Section 3.1 '*The discipline*' to Section 3.10 '*Classroom research and course evaluation*'. It may be sensible at various stages of the re-design for staff to move to a different working group.

By (specify a date) each group is to clearly present on a paper of *x* sides a summary of their discussions on;

- the key features of this approach to curriculum design;
- how aspects of the curriculum in this department could be (re) designed on these lines;
- the main obstacle(s) and how it (they) could be overcome;
- a time scale and methods by which this approach could be implemented.

6 References

6.1 References cited in the text

Abler, R., Adams, J.S., Booker-Gross, S., Conkey, L., Fernald, E., Griffin, E., Mercier, J. & Moline, N. (1994) Reconsidering faculty roles and rewards in geography, *Journal of Geography in Higher Education*, 18(1), pp.7-18.

Agnew, C. & Elton, L. (1998) *Lecturing in Geography* (Cheltenham: Geography Discipline Network, CGCHE).

Alverno College Faculty (1994) *Student Assessment as Learning at Alverno College, Milwaukee*, (Alverno College Faculty).

Angelo, T.A. & Cross, K.T. (1993) *Classroom Assessment Techniques* (San Francisco: Jossey Bass).

Association of American Colleges (AAC) (1985) *Integrity in the College Curriculum: a report to the academic community* (Washington DC: Association of American Colleges).

Backler, A. (1979) Mastery learning: a case study and implications for instruction, *Journal of Geography in Higher Education*, 3(1), pp.68-75.

Banta T.W., Lund J.P., Black K.E. & Oblander F.W. (1996) *Assessment in Practice; putting principles to work on college campuses* (San Francisco: Jossey Bass).

Barff, R. (1995) Small classes and research experience for new undergraduates, *Journal of Geography in Higher Education*, 19(3), pp.299-306.

Becher, T. (1989) *Academic Tribes and Territories* (Milton Keynes: Open University Press).

Bein, F.L. & East (1981) Teaching Geography on Weekends and at Shopping Malls, *Journal of Geography in Higher Education*, 5(2), pp.169-174.

Birnie, J. & Mason O'Connor, K. (1998) *Practicals and Laboratory Work in Geography* (Cheltenham: Geography Discipline Network, CGCHE).

Bloom, B.A. (1956) *Taxonomy of Educational Objectives* (New York: David McKay).

Blumhof, J., Honeybone, A., Pearlman, D. & Pinn, K. (1995) Researchers of our own teaching: theory into practice in the evolution of a teaching and learning strategy for an interdisciplinary environmental studies degree, in: G. Gibbs (Ed.) *Improving Student Learning*, pp.311-322 (Oxford: Oxford Centre for Staff Development).

Boulton-Lewis, G.M. (1995) The solo taxonomy as a means of sharing and assessing learning in higher education, *Higher Education Research and Development*, 14(2), pp.143-154.

Boyer, E.L. (1990) *Scholarship Reconsidered: priorities of the professoriate* (Princeton: Carnegie Foundation).

Bradbeer, J. (1996) Problem-based learning and fieldwork: a better method of preparation, *Journal of Geography in Higher Education*, 20(1), pp.11-18.

Bradford, M. (1996) Regulation of geographical education: present competition and future collaboration, *Journal of Geography in Higher Education*, 20(3), pp. 277-280.

Bradford, M. & O'Connell, C. (1998) *Assessment in Geography* (Cheltenham: Geography Discipline Network, CGCHE).

Bramley, W. & Wood, P. (1982) Collaboration, consultation and conflict: the process of change in a teaching department, *Journal of Geography in Higher Education*, 6(1), pp.5-20.

Brew, A. & Boud, D. (1995) Teaching and Research: stabilising the vital link with learning, *Higher Education*, 29, pp.261-273.

Bryson, J. (1997) Breaking through the A-level effect: a first year tutorial in student self-reflection, *Journal of Geography in Higher Education*, 21(2), pp.163-170.

Buckingham-Hatfield, S. (1995) Student-community partnerships: advocating community enterprise projects in geography, *Journal of Geography in Higher Education*, 19(2), pp.143-150.

Bunge, W. (1971) *Fitzgerald — Geography of a Revolution* (Cambridge Massachusetts: Schenkman).

Burkill, S (1997) Student empowerment through group work: a case study, *Journal of Geography in Higher Education*, 21(1), pp.89 –94.

Centra, J.A. (1993) *Reflective Faculty Evaluation Enhancing Teaching and Determining Faculty Effectiveness* (San Francisco: Jossey-Bass).

Chalkley, B. (1996) Geography and teaching quality assessment: how well did we do?, *Journal of Geography in Higher Education*, 20(2) pp.149-158.

Chalkley, B. & Harwood, J. (1998) *Transferable Skills and Work-based Learning in Geography* (Cheltenham: Geography Discipline Network, CGCHE).

Chapman, K. (1994) Variability of degree results in Geography in United Kingdom universities, 1973-90: preliminary results and policy implications, *Studies in Higher Education*, 19(1), pp.89-102.

Chapman, K. (1996) An analysis of degree results in geography by gender, *Assessment & Evaluation in Higher Education*, 21(4), pp.293-311.

Chapman, K. (1997) Changing assessment practices in first and second year geography modules using computer-assisted assessment (CAA) to set formative and summative objective tests, http://www.chelt.ac.uk/gdn/abstracts/a40.htm.

Cho, G. (1982) Experiences with a workbook for spatial data-analysis, *Journal of Geography in Higher Education*, 6(2) pp.133-139.

Clark, D., Healey, M.J. & Kennedy, R. (1990) Careers for Geographers: the experience of Coventry Polytechnic sandwich degree students, *Journal of Geography in Higher Education*, 14(1), pp.137-150.

Cook, R.U. (1992) Common ground, shared inheritance: reserach imperatives for environmental geography, *Transactions of the Institute of British Geographers, New Series*, 17, pp.131-151.

Corbridge, S. (1985) The green revolution game, *Journal of Geography in Higher Education*, 9(2) pp.171-175.

Cosgrove, D. (1981) Teaching geographical thought through student interviews, *Journal of Geography in Higher Education*, 5(1) pp.19-22.

Cross, K.P. & Steadman, M.H. (1996) *Classroom Research: implementing the scholarship of teaching* (San Francisco: Jossey-Bass).

DES (1992) *A Survey of Geography Fieldwork in Degree Courses* (Stanmore: Department of Education and Science).

Dawson, B., Dent, D., Davidson, D., Nortcliff, S. & FitzPatrick, E.A. (1995) Soil Surveyor, in: S.B. Heath (Ed.) *MERTaL(TM) Courseware* (Aberdeen: University of Aberdeen).

de Vries, P. (1996) Could 'criteria' used in quality assessments be classified as academic standards?, *Higher Education Quarterly*, 3, July, pp.193-206.

Diamond, R.M. (1989) *Designing and Improving Courses and Curricula in Higher Education: a systematic approach* (San Francisco: Jossey-Bass).

Diamond, R.M. & Adam, B.E. (1993) Recognising faculty work: reward systems for the year 2000, *New Directions for Higher Education*, 81 (San Francisco: Jossey Bass).

Dressel, P.L.R. & Marcus, D. (1982) *On Teaching and Learning in College* (San Francisco: Jossey-Bass).

Evans, C. (1993) *The Experience of Teaching and Learning English in British Universities* (Milton Keynes: Open University Press).

Forbes, D. & Spence, J. (1991) An experiment in assessment for a large class, in: R. Smith (Ed.) *Innovations in Teaching Engineering*, pp.97-101 (London: Ellis Horwood).

Fox, M. & Wilkinson, T. (1977) A self-paced instruction scheme in geography for a first-year introductory course, *Journal of Geography in Higher Education*, 1(2), pp.61-70.

Fox, M., Rowsome, W.S. & Wilkinson, T. (1987) A decade of mastery learning: evolution and evaluation, *Journal of Geography in Higher Education*, 11(1), pp.11-26.

Gibbs, G. (1992a) *Improving the Quality of Student Learning* (Bristol: Technical and Educational Services).

Gibbs, G. (1992b) *Independent Learning with More Students*. Teaching More Students No. 5 (Oxford: Oxford Centre for Staff Development).

Gibbs, G. (1992c) *Problems and Course Design Strategies*. Teaching More Students No. 1 (Oxford: Oxford Centre for Staff Development).

Gibbs, G. (1992d) *Assessing More Students*. Teaching More Students No. 4 (Oxford: Oxford Centre for Staff Development).

Gibbs, G. (1994a) Learning from Alverno, in: Walker, L. (Ed.) *Institutional Change Towards Ability–based Curriculum in Higher Education*, pp.29-37 (Oxford: Oxford Brookes, Department of Employment).

Gibbs, G. (1994b) *Learning in Teams: Student Guide* (Oxford: Oxford Centre for Staff Development).

Gibbs, G., Gregory, R. & Moore, I. (1997) *Laboratories and Practicals with More Students* (Oxford: Oxford Centre for Staff Development).

Gold, J., Jenkins, A., Lee, R., Monk, J., Riley, D., Shepherd, I. & Unwin, D. (1991) *Teaching Geography in Higher Education: a manual of good practice* (Oxford: Blackwell).

Goodall, B. (1977) Problems arising from the use of continuous assessment for degree classification, *Journal of Geography in Higher Education*, 1(1), pp.47-52.

Gould, P. (1973) The open geographic curriculum, in: R.J. Chorley, (Ed.) *Directions in Geography*, pp.253-84 (London: Methuen).

Graff, J.G. (1991) _New Life for the College Curriculum_ (San Francisco: Jossey-Bass).

Green, T. (1998) _Publishing Single Field: students guide_ (Oxford: Oxford Brookes University).

Haigh, M.J. (1986) The evaluation of an experiment in physical geography teaching, _Journal of Geography in Higher Education_, 10(2), pp.133-47.

Haines-Young, R.H. (1983) Nutrient cycling and problem solving: a simple teaching model, _Journal of Geography in Higher Education_, 7(2), pp.125-39.

Hancock, D. (1986) The future of geography in Higher Education, _Institute of British Geographers Annual Conference, Reading_, unpublished paper.

Hansen, E., Kennedy, S., Mattingly, D., Mitchneck, B., Monzel, K. & Nairne, C. (1995) Facing the future, surviving the present: strategies for women graduate students in geography, _Journal of Geography in Higher Education_, 19(3), pp.307-316.

Harrison, M.E. (1995) Images of the Third World: teaching a geography of the Third World, _Journal of Geography in Higher Education_, 19(3), pp.285-299.

Healey, M., Matthews, H., Livingstone, I. & Foster, I. (1996) Learning in small groups in university geography courses: designing a core module, _Journal of Geography in Higher Education_, 20(2), pp.167-180.

Healey, M. (1997) Geography and education: perspectives on quality in UK higher education, _Progress in Human Geography_, 21(1), pp.97-108.

Higher Education Funding Council for England (HEFCE) (1995a) _Quality Assessment for Geography_ 1994-5, Subject Overview Report (Bristol: HEFCE).

Higher Education Funding Council for England (HEFCE) (1995b) _Quality Assessment Report by the HEFCE for University College London, Geography_ (Bristol: HEFCE).

Higher Education Funding Council for England (HEFCE) (1995c) _Report on Quality Assessment, 1992-5_ (Bristol: HEFCE).

Higher Education Quality Council (HEQC) (1996) _Modular Higher Education in the UK_ (London: HEQC).

Higher Education Quality Council (HEQC) (1997a) _Academic Digest_ (London: HEQC).

Higher Education Quality Council (HEQC) (1997b) _Quality, Standards and Professional Accreditation_ (London: HEQC).

Higher Education Quality Council (HEQC) (1997c) _The Graduates Standards Programme, Final Report_ (London: HEQC).

Hounsell, D. (1997) Understanding teaching and teaching for understanding, in: F. Marton, Hounsell, D. & Entwistle, N. (Eds.) _The Experience of Learning_, pp.238-257 (Edinburgh: Scottish Academic Press).

Jackson, N. (1997) Implications of the Dearing Report for Academic Standards in Geoscience Education, _Geoscientist_, 7(10), pp.9-15.

Jackson, N. (1998) _Programme specifications and their potential role in creating a more explicit environment for demonstrating, recording and reporting achievement_, unpublished paper.

Jackson, P. (1996) Only connect: approaches to human geography, in: E. Rawling & R.A. Daugherty (Eds.) _Geography into the Twenty-First Century_, pp.77-94 (London: Wiley).

Jenkins, A. (1992) Encouraging active learning in structured lectures, in: G. Gibbs (Ed.) *Improving the Quality of Student Learning* (Bristol: Technical & Education Services).

Jenkins, A. (1997) *Fieldwork with More Students* (Oxford: Oxford Centre for Staff Development).

Jenkins, A., Blackman, T., Lindsay, R. & Paton-Saltzberg, R. (1998) Teaching and research: student perspectives and policy implications, *Studies in Higher Education*, 23(2), pp.127-142.

Jenkins, A. & Smith, P. (1993) Expansion, efficiency and effectiveness: the experience of British geography departments, *Transactions of the Institute of British Geographers, New Series*, 18, pp.500-515.

Johnson, H.G. (1995) The National Geography Standards and your undergraduate curriculum: the opportunity that knocks more than once, *Journal of Geography*, Sept / Oct, pp.534-537.

Johnson, J.R. & Oliver, M. (1991) Urban poverty and social welfare policy in the United States: an undergraduate research/training programme, *Journal of Geography in Higher Education*, 15(1), pp.25-34.

Johnston, R. (1996) And now it's all over, was it worth all the effort?, *Journal of Geography in Higher Education*, 20(2) pp.159-165.

Jumper, S. (1992) Progam assessment in geography: boondoggle or opportunity, *Journal of Geography*, 91(3), pp.94-96.

Kakela, P. (1979) Remembering teaching, *Journal of Geography in Higher Education*, 3(1), pp.5-12.

Keller, F.S. & Sherman, J.C. (1974) *The Keller Plan Handbook: essays on a personalised system of instruction* (Menlo Park, CA: Benjamin).

King, R. (1976) Assessment in geography: approaches to the formulation of objectives, *Studies in Higher Education*, 3(1), pp.223-232.

Kirk, R.M. (1995) Editorial: Geography as conversation, *Journal of Geography in Higher Education*, 19(3), pp.269-270.

Kinsman, B. (1965) *Wind Waves, their Generation and Propagation on the Ocean Surface* (Prentice-Hall).

Kneale, P. (1997) Maximising play time: time management for geography students, *Journal of Geography in Higher Education*, 21(2), pp.293 -301.

Laurillard, D. (1993) *Rethinking University Teaching: a framework for the effective use of educational technology* (London: Routledge).

Laurillard, D. (1997) Learning formal representations through multimedia, in: D. Hounsell, F. Marton & N. Entwistle (Eds.) *The Experience of Learning*, pp.172-183 (Edinburgh: Scottish Academic Press).

Leftwich, A. (1987) Room for manoeuvre: a report on experiments in alternative teaching and learning methods in politics, *Studies in Higher Education*, 12(3), pp.311-323.

Lineback, N.G. & Harlin, J.M. (1987) *Physical Geography Lab Manual: a new experimental approach* (Dubuque: Kendall Hunt).

Livingstone, I., Matthews, H. & Castley, A. (1998) *Fieldwork and Dissertations in Geography* (Cheltenham: Geography Discipline Network, CGCHE).

Longworth, D. (1994) Crediting students for helping students, in: A. Jenkins & Walker, L. (Eds.) *Developing Student Capability Through Modular Courses*, pp.95-100 (London: Kogan Page).

McDowell, L. (1992) Engendering Change: curriculum transformation in human geography, *Journal of Geography in Higher Education*, 16(2), pp.185-198.

McKernan, J. (1996) *Curriculum Action Research*, 2nd Edition (London: Kogan Page).

Mohan, J. (1995) Thinking local: service learning, education for citizenship and geography, *Journal of Geography in Higher Education*, 19(2), pp.129-142.

Murray, H.G. (1997) Does evaluation of teaching lead to improvement of teaching? *The International Journal for Academic Development*, 2(1), pp.8-23.

National Committee of Inquiry into Higher Education (1997) *Higher Education in the Learning Society: The Dearing Report* (London: HMSO).

O'Riordan, T. (1981) Environmentalism and education, *Journal of Geography in Higher Education*, 5(1), pp.3-18.

O'Riordan, T. (1996) Environmentalism and geography: a union still to be consummated, in: E. Rawling & R.A. Daugherty (Eds.) *Geography into the Twenty-First Century*, pp.113-128 (London: Wiley).

Oliver, S. (1995) Empowering student learning with supplemental instruction, in: A. Jenkins & A. Ward (Eds.) *Developing Skill Based Curricula through the Disciplines: case studies of good practice in geography*, pp. 97-101 (Birmingham: Staff and Educational Development Association).

Parlett, M. (1977) The department as a learning milieu, *Studies in Higher Education*, 2, pp.173-181.

Pascarella, E.T. & Terenzini, P.T. (1991) *How College Affects Students* (San Francisco: Jossey Bass).

Pepper, D.M. (1987 Physical and human integration: an educational perspective from British Higher Education, *Progress in Human Geography*, 11(3), pp.379-404.

Pepper, D.M. & Webster, F. (1998) *The Assessment of Undergraduate Dissertations in the School of Social Sciences and Law* (Oxford: Oxford Brookes University, internal report).

Phillips, M. & Healey, M. (1996) Teaching the history and philosophy of geography, *Journal of Geography in Higher Education*, 20(2), pp.223-242.

Pirsig, R.M. (1976) *Zen and the Art of Motorcycle Maintenance: an inquiry into values* (Corgi Edition).

Powell, J. (1990) Australian geography and the corporate management paradigm, *Journal of Geography in Higher Education*, 14(1), pp.5-18.

QAA (1998) *An Agenda for Quality* (Gloucester: QAA).

Ramsden, P. (1992) *Learning to Teach in Higher Education* (London: Routledge).

Rich, D.C., Pitman, A.J., Gosper, M. & Jacobson, C. (1997) Restructuring of Australian higher education: information technology in geography teaching and learning, *Australian Geographer*, 28(2), pp.135-157.

Rowntree, D. (1974) *Educational Technology in Curriculum Development* (London: Harper & Row).

Rowntree, D. (1981) *Developing Courses for Students*, Revised Edition (London: McGraw-Hill).

Sacks, P. (1996) *Generation X Goes to College* (Chicago: Open Court).

Sauer, C.O. (1956) The education of a geographer, *Annals of the Association of American Geographers*, 46, pp.287-99.

Shepherd, I. (1998) *Teaching and Learning Geography with Information and Communication Technologies* (Cheltenham: Geography Discipline Network, CGCHE).

Smith, D.M. (1995) Moral teaching in geography, *Journal of Geography in Higher Education*, 19(3), pp.271-284.

Snyder, B.R. (1971) *The Hidden Curriculum* (New York: Knopf).

Squires, G. (1987) The curriculum, in: T. Becher (Ed.) *British Higher Education*, pp.155-177 (London: Allen & Unwin).

Stark, J.S. & Luttaca, J.S. (1996) *Shaping the College Curriculum: Academic Plans in Action* (Boston: Allyn & Brown).

Strachan, A. (1984) Bridging the gap between school and college: evidence from the University of Leicester 1978-82, *Journal of Geography in Higher Education*, 8(2), pp.125-136.

Thomas, K. (1990) *Gender and Subject in Higher Education* (Milton Keynes: Open University Press).

Trow, M. (1976) The American academic department as a context for learning, *Studies in Higher Education*, 1, pp.11-22.

Unwin, T. (1986) Attitudes towards geographers in the graduate labour market, *Journal of Geography in Higher Education*, 16(2), pp.149-158.

Unwin, T. (1997) Rotten to the core: against a core curriculum for geography in UK higher education, *Journal of Geography in Higher Education*, 21(2), pp.252-260.

Walker, L. (Ed.) (1994) *Institutional Change towards Ability–based Curriculum in Higher Education* (Oxford: Oxford Brookes, Department of Employment).

Wagenaar, T.C. (1993) The Capstone Course: a special issue, *Teaching Sociology*, 21(3), pp.209-214.

Wilson, K.L., Lizzio, A. & Ramsden, P. (1997) The development, validation and application of the course experience questionnaire, *Studies in Higher Education*, 22(1), pp.33-53.

Wood, P. (1980) The undergraduate teaching review, 1987-1980, *Occasional Paper 37, Department of Geography* (London: University College London).

Wright, P. (1996) Mass higher education and the search for standards: reflections on some issues emerging from the Graduate Standards Programme, *Higher Education Quarterly*, 50(1), pp.71-85.

6.2 Guide to other sources

6.2.1   Books and journals

Generic (i.e. relevant to all disciplines)

Angelo, T.A. & Cross, K.T. (1993) *Classroom Assessment Techniques* (San Francisco: Jossey Bass).

> A superb compendium of how college teachers can research their student understanding of what is being taught and revise their courses to improve that understanding.

Diamond, R.M. (1989) *Designing and Improving Courses and Curricula in Higher Education: a systematic approach* (San Francisco: Jossey-Bass).

> Written from the perspective that there is powerful and systematic way to design courses. The view is that this is best done by design specialists working for discipline-based staff. Based on work at Syracuse University.

Gibbs, G. (1992) *Improving the Quality of Student Learning* (Bristol: Technical and Educational Services).

> The results of an action research project, where an educational developer, (Gibbs) worked with staff from a range of disciplines including geography to redesign their courses to develop deep learning.

Gibbs, G. (1992) *Problems and Strategic Options.* Teaching More Students No. 1 (Oxford: Oxford Centre for Staff Development).

> A practical manual that considers the particular issues and strategies for designing large courses.

Pascarella, E.T. & Terenzini, P.T. (1991) *How College Affects Students* (San Francisco: Jossey Bass).

> This Guide has only partly indicated the research evidence on which it is based. This book is a comprehensive review of the research evidence on college learning.

Stark, J.S. & Latuca, J.S. (1997) *Shaping the College Curriculum: academic plans in action* (Boston: Allyn and Bacon).

> A comprehensive and scholarly account of US practice and research,

Rowntree, D. (1985) *Developing Courses for Students*, Revised Edition (London: McGraw-Hill).

> Clearly aimed at curriculum design in higher education; takes one through key issues in a scholarly and practical manner.

Geography Specific

Gould, P. (1973) The Open Geographic Curriculum, in: R.J. Chorley (Ed.) *Directions in Geography*, pp.253-284 (London: Methuen).

> A classic article by someone who has been a leader in the discipline and on discussions of teaching. Written from both a US and a European perspective. We may not agree with its particular perspective — thus Gould sees physical geography as a separate intellectual field from human geography and mathematics is seen as central; the article will help us to articulate what we believe.

Hindle, B.P. (1993) The 'Project': putting student-controlled small-group work and transferable skills at the core of a geography course, *Journal of Geography in Higher Education*, 17(1), pp.11-20.

> An account of a fundamental redesign of a first year programme, to create a large common project-based course around local issues and developing key transferable skills.

Jenkins, A. (1992) Encouraging active learning in structured lectures, in: G. Gibbs (Ed.) *Improving the Quality of Student Learning*, (Bristol: Technical & Education Services).

> How a large first year lecture based course was re-designed to develop deep learning.

Pepper, D.M. (1987 Physical and human integration: an educational perspective from British Higher Education, *Progress in Human Geography*, 11(3), pp.379-404.

> David Pepper, whose research interests started in physical geography and who now researches environmental philosophy has been central to creating the integrated perspective outlined in case study 4.3. Here he argues for the importance of integrating physical and human geography but argues this will require a particular socially relevant conception of physical geography at undergraduate level.

Sauer, C.O. (1956) The education of a geographer, *Annals of the Association of American Geographers*, 46, pp.287-99.

> Simply a classic and a powerful, if perhaps dated, argument for the central role of fieldwork in the geography curriculum.

6.2.2   WWW sites

Geography Discipline Network

http://www.chelt.ac.uk/gdn/

> The WWW site for the Geography Discipline Network project. This contains brief descriptions on many aspects of geography teaching, and an invitation for you to contribute case studies. Abstracts from the *Journal of Geography in Higher Education* can also be accessed from the GDN pages.

Geography Departments

http://www.geog.gla.ac.uk/sites/geogsites.htm

> The curricula/course descriptions, staff, etc. of other geography departments world-wide can be reached through this site (part of the Virtual Geography Department — see below)

http://www.hefce.ac.uk/

> This WWW site of the Higher Education Funding Council for England contains all the reports of the geography subject assessors on the geography departments assessed in the 1994 Geography TQA (reports are at http://back.niss.ac.uk/education/hefce/qar/geography.html)

http://www.utexas.edu/depts/grg/virtdept/contents.html

> The Virtual Geography Department. This is a developing world-wide Internet-based sources and curricula materials (see Section 4.4).

http://www.ncgia.ucsb.edu/education/ed.html

The shape of things to come? As well as the virtual geography department there are other developing WWW-based curricula materials in geography. This is the site of the NCGIA Core Curriculum in GIS — which provides key course content written by leading experts world-wide for adapting to local courses is at http://bbq.ncgia.ucsb.edu:80/giscc/

Professional Geography Organisations

Many of the national geography societies have study groups and publications on geography in higher education. Relevant WWW sites include:

http://www.aag.org/default.htm

Association of American Geographers (see Geography Education Speciality Group). Note this web site also gives details on the curricula materials and modules being developed through the Human Dimensions of Global Change Project by Clark University, directed by Susan Hanson.

http://www.ssn.flinders.edu.au/geog/iag/welcome.htm

Institute of Australian Geographers

http://www.uwindsor.ca/cag/

Canadian Association of Geographers

http://multimedia2.freac.fsu.edu/ncge/

National Council for Geographic Education (USA)

Information Technology and Geography Curricula

http://www.geog.le.ac.uk/cti/

CTI (Computers in Teaching Initiative for Geography, Geology and Metereology)

http://www.abo.fi/hied/

Higher Education Development International (HIED) is a meta-WWW site that brings together a wide collection of WWW sites and materials concerned with many aspects of teaching in higher education.

http://www.lgu.ac.uk/deliberations/

DeLiberations is an electronic journal concerned with many aspects of teaching in higher education including geography.

6.2.3 Video

'*A Private Universe*', Pyramid Films and Video, 2801 Colorado Avenue, Santa Monica, California, 9404, USA.

See the description in Section 3.4 of the first few minutes of this eighteen minute video. Produced as part of a high school science reform project most of it follows one bright student trying to link her private universe with what she is learning in school. The first few minutes are well worth seeing...